# AN INTRODUCTION TO ORCHIDS

SOUTH FLORIDA ORCHID SOCIETY

INCORPORATED

*South Florida Orchid Society*
*June 2000*

Edited by
Dr. Ruben P. Sauleda
Leonard A. Sandow
Charles J. Ochipa

© Copyright 1997 by The South Florida Orchid Society

ISBN 0-9679831-0-X

Designed and printed by: **American Printing Arts, Incorporated**
Art Director: **Robin Foote, American Printing Arts, Incorporated**

Editors: **Dr. Ruben P. Sauleda, Leonard A. Sandow, Charles J. Ochipa**

Illustrations: **Rebeka Sauleda**

Contributors:

| | |
|---|---|
| Introduction | Dr. Ruben P. Sauleda |
| Pests and Diseases | Dr. Ruben P. Sauleda |
| Nutrition | Dr. Ruben P. Sauleda |
| Propagation | Dr. Ruben P. Sauleda |
| Classification | Dr. Ruben P. Sauleda |
| Removing Seedlings from Flasks | Kenneth Cameron |
| Cattleya | William A. Peters II |
| Vandaceous | Robert Fuchs |
| Dendrobiums | Lynn Bretsnyder |
| Phalaenopsis | Leonard A. Sandow |
| Lady Slippers | Gene Monnier |
| Oncidiinae | Dr. Berton C. Pressman |
| Catasetinae | Dr. Berton C. Pressman |
| Terrestrials | Kerry Richards |
| Florida Orchids | Dr. Ruben P. Sauleda |

Other Contributors: Robert C. Randall, Drago Strahija, Tim Anderson, Milton Carpenter, Charles J. Ochipa and Dorothy Bennet

Photographic Credits: Leonard A. Sandow, Dr. Ruben P. Sauleda, Robert Fuchs, Charles J. Ochipa, Gene Monnier, Kenneth Cameron, Maria T. Mascareñas, Drago Strahija, Francisco Miranda, Lynn Bretsnyder, Kerry Richards, William A. Peters, II

Cover:  Blc. Alma Kee, photograph by *Leonard A. Sandow*
　　　　grown by *Maria T. Mascareñas*

# TABLE OF CONTENTS

# INTRODUCTORY LETTER FROM THE PRESIDENT

The Board of Directors of the South Florida Orchid Society is proud to announce the reprinting of an Introduction to Growing Orchids. The first printing has been an

Aranda Noorah Alsagoff (pink)

enormous success, selling out much sooner than we anticipated. All of the feedback we have heard from amateur growers has been positive.

This book represents the long and hard work of many of the professional growers and some advanced hobby growers. We hope that this reprinted volume will continue to be a source of information that contributes to the better understanding

and enjoyment of the hobby of growing orchids.

Happy orchid growing.

Dr. Ruben P. Sauleda

# GROWING ORCHIDS

### What is an Orchid – How Do Orchids Differ From Other Plants?

Orchids are distinguished from other plants by a combination of three characters which are not found together in any other plant family. These distinguishing characters are:

- Pollen is joined into a mass and called a pollinarium (pollina pl.)
- Stamens and pistils are joined into a structure called a column
- Seeds are very tiny containing no endosperm and no organized embryo

All of these characters are found individually in other plant families, but not collectively.

### Size of Orchid Family

Orchids are the largest family of flowering plants. Ten percent of all the flowering plants on earth are orchids.

Orchids are divided into 800 genera and 35,000 to 50,000 valid species. In addition there are thousands of artificial, man-made hybrids. Thousands of new hybrids are being made annually by both commercial and amateur growers.

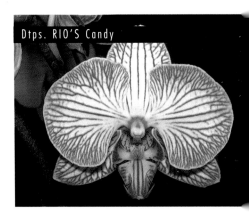

Dtps. RIO'S Candy

Ascda. John De Biase

Lc. Mildred Rives

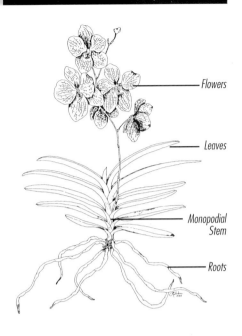

Flowers

Leaves

Monopodial Stem

Roots

## Morpology of the Orchid Plant

Orchids exhibit two types of growth: Sympodial and monopodial.

Sympodial plants have growth along a rhizome with new growth arising from the base of the previous growth. Most of these plants have upright leafy stems or pseudobulbs bearing leaves. Inflorescences arise from apex or base of stem or pseudobulb.

Monopodial plants have growth along a stem from which leaves arise apically. The inflorescences are produced laterally from between the leaves.

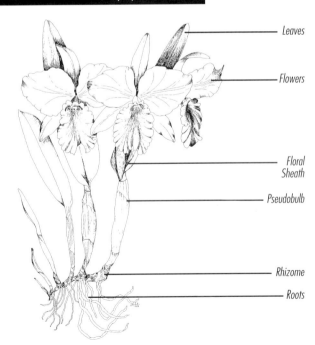

Leaves

Flowers

Floral Sheath

Pseudobulb

Rhizome

Roots

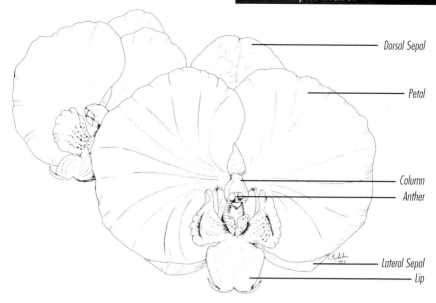

Dorsal Sepal

Petal

Column
Anther

Lateral Sepal
Lip

## Morphology of the Orchid Flower

The part of the plant bearing the flowers is called an inflorescence. The individual flower consists of the pedicel, the sepals, petals, labellum and column. The pedicel is the stem of the flower and includes the ovary which contains the ovules or eggs. The floral segments are in threes, three sepals and three petals. Orchids have a dorsal sepal and two lateral sepals. In addition orchids have three petals, however, two are similar and the third is modified into a labellum or lip. This lip usually encloses the column and functions to attract pollinators. The column contains the reproductive parts. At the apex of the column is the anther containing the pollen and directly behind the anther is the stigmatic surface.

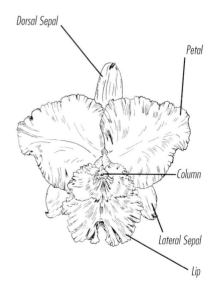

Dorsal Sepal

Petal

Column

Lateral Sepal

Lip

# Choosing Your First Orchid

C. loddigesii

Den. Candy Stripe

Phal. Sarah's Sunset

Choosing your first orchid is critical to your future as an orchid grower. If it does not grow you will be discouraged and miss out in what is probably the most rewarding hobby known to man. Growing orchids can give you hours of relaxing pleasure and a tremendous sense of pride when that first seedling that you have grown for several years flowers. Sometimes just flowering a difficult to grow orchid can be rewarding.

The choice of your first orchid should be a careful choice based on the conditions you will be growing your orchids in. Usually you can control most of the elements needed for good orchid growing: light, temperature, aeration, water and nutrition. Many times however there are one or two elements you can not control. If you are growing on the north side of your house the light available will be very low. If you are growing on the south side of your house the light available will be strong. If you live in an area where there are strong winds then your plants will dry rapidly, conversely if you have poor air circulation your plants will remain damp. A combination of low light and poor air circulation can make it very difficult to grow most types of orchids.

Dendrobiums are found for sale in just about every garden department and are inexpensive. If you purchase one they need strong light, frequent watering and good air circulation. Phalaenopsis are perfect for low light situations but need good air circulation. Cattleyas need strong light and good air circulation.

Exposure to cold temperatures is also a major consideration. Some species of dendrobiums not only like cold temperatures but actually require them to flower. Other dendrobiums like the ones commonly found for sale in garden departments do not tolerate low temperatures. Cattleyas like cool temperatures, but phalaenopsis are unhappy below 55° F and vandas also get very unhappy with cold temperatures. The choice is yours but be careful, especially with expensive plants. It is always best to experiment with inexpensive plants until you feel confident about growing orchids. Most important of all do not get discouraged.

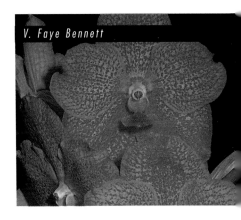
V. Faye Bennett

Oncidium Sunset Fort 'Marilyn Ochipa'

Paph. Angel's Flight

# GENERAL ORCHID CULTURE

This is a general overview of the requirements for cultivating orchids. More details will follow after each specific group.

Light, temperature, water, aeration and nutrition are the five most important elements in cultivating orchids. All five are interrelated and achieving optimum growing conditions requires that each grower find the proper balance between the five elements which best suits their growing conditions. For example, if a grower is growing under strong light then he must water more often to compensate for the higher temperatures which will occur and fertilize more often to compensate for the higher energy requirements the plants will have.

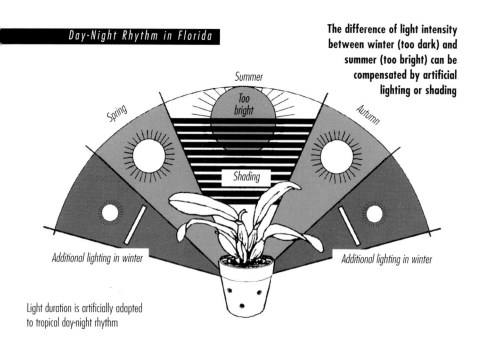

Day-Night Rhythm in Florida

The difference of light intensity between winter (too dark) and summer (too bright) can be compensated by artificial lighting or shading

Spring

Summer

Too bright

Shading

Autumn

Additional lighting in winter

Additional lighting in winter

Light duration is artificially adapted to tropical day-night rhythm

## Light Intensity

Most orchids, with the exception of phalaenopsis which require more shade, will grow well under 60-50% shade. However 65-70% shade is best for mature established cattleyas, 35-50% shade is best for vandas and dendrobiums and 75-80% shade is best for phalaenopsis.

## Light Quality

The red and blue light bands are the most important in photosynthesis, therefore care must be used in the choice of shading materials. Colored plastics or fiberglass filter out desirable light and although the light intensity appears high many plants especially cattleyas and vandas will not grow or flower well.

## Appearance of Well Grown Plants

Plants grown under proper light intensity will have a slightly yellowish cast, hard leathery textured leaves, red or purple pigment in the leaves, pseudobulb and flower sheath, and produce sugar droplets on the new growths.

**Changing Conditions Over the Year**

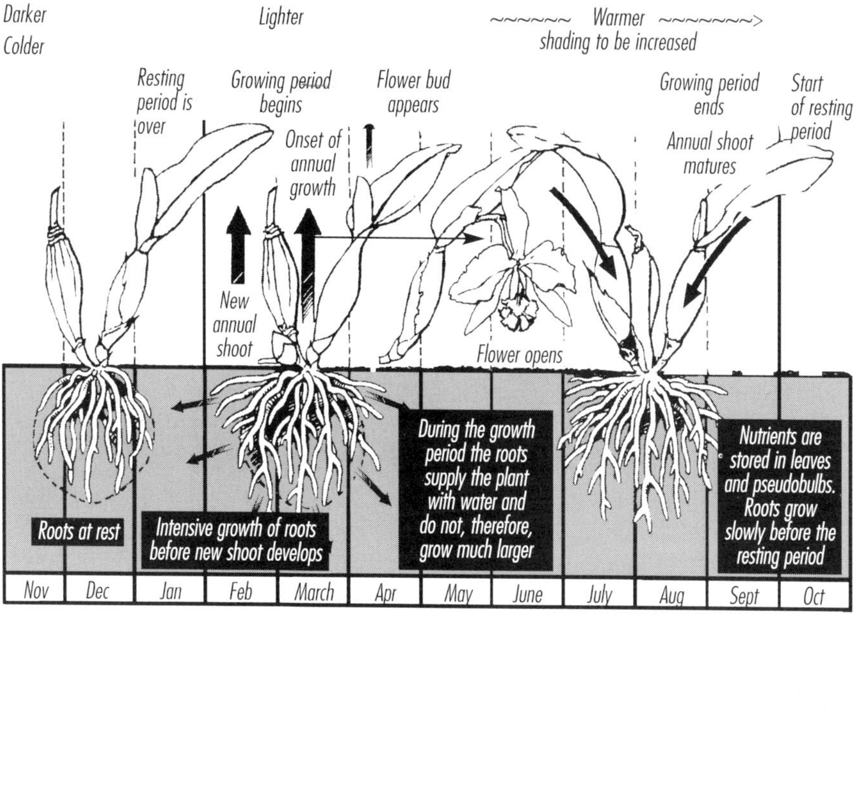

Darker Colder

Lighter

~~~~~ Warmer ~~~~~~~>
shading to be increased

Resting period is over

Growing period begins

Flower bud appears

Onset of annual growth

Growing period ends

Start of resting period

Annual shoot matures

New annual shoot

Flower opens

Roots at rest

Intensive growth of roots before new shoot develops

During the growth period the roots supply the plant with water and do not, therefore, grow much larger

Nutrients are stored in leaves and pseudobulbs. Roots grow slowly before the resting period

| Nov | Dec | Jan | Feb | March | Apr | May | June | July | Aug | Sept | Oct |

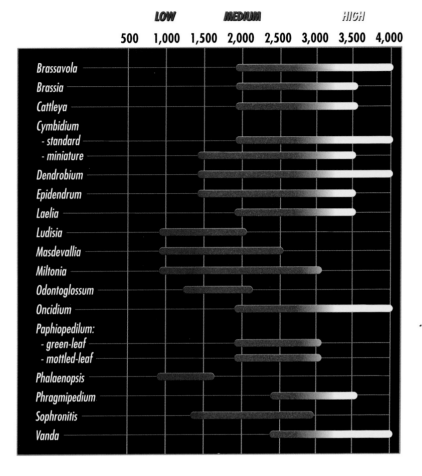

| | LOW | | MEDIUM | | | HIGH | |
|---|---|---|---|---|---|---|---|
| | 500 | 1,000 | 1,500 | 2,000 | 2,500 | 3,000 | 3,500 | 4,000 |

Brassavola
Brassia
Cattleya
Cymbidium
- standard
- miniature
Dendrobium
Epidendrum
Laelia
Ludisia
Masdevallia
Miltonia
Odontoglossum
Oncidium
Paphiopedilum:
- green-leaf
- mottled-leaf
Phalaenopsis
Phragmipedium
Sophronitis
Vanda

## TEMPERATURE

Temperature affects photosynthesis, respiration and flowering.

Photosynthesis, which is the production and storage of energy by the plant, is inhibited below 40° F and above 110° F. The optimum for biological reactions in the plant is 75-80° F.

Respiration is the process by which energy is used by the cell, at high temperatures the plant requires energy faster than it can produce it resulting in severe burning of the leaves.

Temperature also plays a key role in the initiation of flower spikes in phalaenopsis. Several nights of low temperatures are required for the initiation of flower spikes. The quality of the flower is also determined by the temperature during bud development. During hot weather the bud will open faster and result in smaller flowers. During the winter, buds will take much longer to develop resulting in larger and better quality flowers.

## Controlling Temperature

Temperatures in a greenhouse can be lowered by reducing the light intensity. However, this upsets the balance and results in having to change the watering and fertilizing patterns. Raising the humidity by adding sprinklers under the bench or simply flooding the area under the plants is probably the best method. Other methods include the installation of wet pads and fans, however this can be costly. Light misting of plants during the hottest time of day is effective but the plants must be dry before dark or the risk of disease will be high.

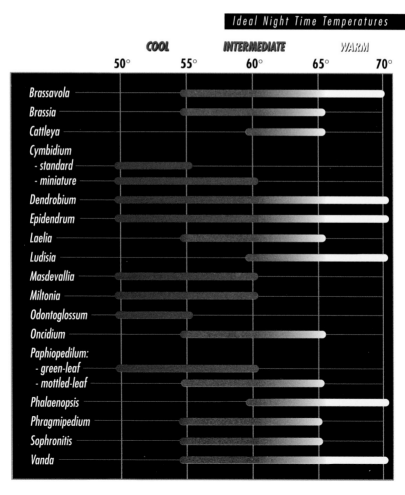

Ideal Night Time Temperatures

# WATER

Humidity is the gaseous water in the air. Low humidity increases transpiration causing dehydration and severely stressing the plants. Optimum humidity is 50-80% of saturation.

Plants should be pot-watered insuring a thorough soaking, once a week to twice a day depending on humidity. The plant should dry between waterings, however the medium should remain slightly moist and never become completely dry. The amount of watering required will vary from season to season. Usually during the winter plants will not dry as quickly as during the summer. Plants which require watering every day during the summer may only require watering once a week during winter.

Always maintain a regular watering pattern. The root system of a plant develops depending on the watering pattern. Vandas will maintain a short compact root system with proper watering. Under watering will result in unnecessarily long roots which will be damaged if the watering pattern is changed and the plants are overwatered.

**Influences of Moisture**

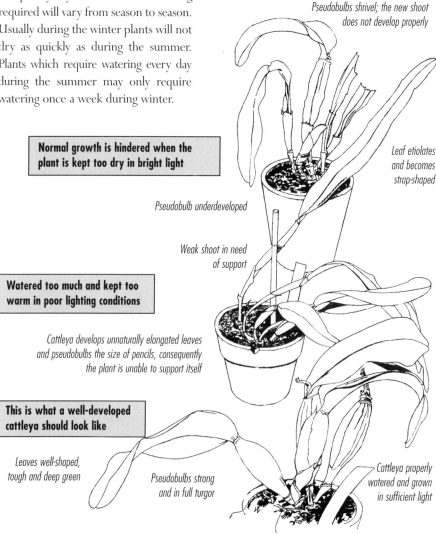

Pseudobulbs shrivel; the new shoot does not develop properly

**Normal growth is hindered when the plant is kept too dry in bright light**

Leaf etiolates and becomes strap-shaped

Pseudobulb underdeveloped

Weak shoot in need of support

**Watered too much and kept too warm in poor lighting conditions**

Cattleya develops unnaturally elongated leaves and pseudobulbs the size of pencils, consequently the plant is unable to support itself

**This is what a well-developed cattleya should look like**

Leaves well-shaped, tough and deep green

Pseudobulbs strong and in full turgor

Cattleya properly watered and grown in sufficient light

## Aeration

Proper air circulation is necessary to dry the leaves and the medium and to remove noxious gases. The vegetative part of the plants should always dry approximately 3-4 hours after watering. If they do not then the air circulation must be increased. If the plants do not dry rapidly or remain wet overnight bacterial diseases will usually infect the plants.

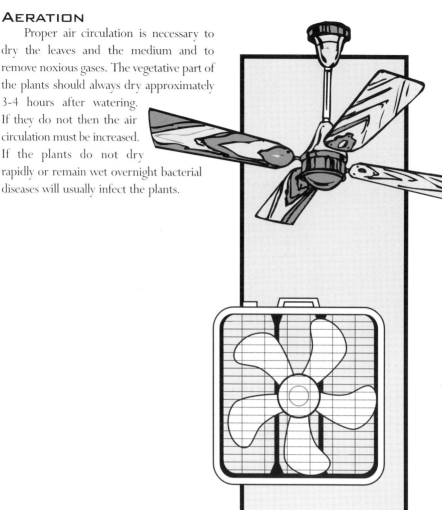

# GROWING ORCHIDS UNDER TREES OR ATTACHED TO TREES

Cattleya aurantiaca

Dendrobium jenkensii

We are fortunate in South Florida that the weather is mild enough that orchids can be attached to trees or grown in containers under trees. The best trees to attach orchids directly to are oak, mango, avocado and citrus. Oaks are probably the best. Mango, avocado and citrus are also very good because orchids seem to attach easily. On many trees orchids appear to attach immediately but after a time the orchids do not seem to like the tree and the roots usually die. Mango, avocado and citrus trees harbor scale and white fly which produce a secretion that causes a black fungus to grow on the leaves of the orchids. This fungus is not only unsightly but will reduce the amount of light reaching the leaves and interfere with the growth of the plants.

Most plants can be attached directly to the trees or some root dressing can be used. Osmunda or sphagnum moss around the roots can help to accelerate the rooting process.

Due to our mild climate many orchids can be hung under trees. Plants which require less light can be hung towards the center of the tree. Plants which prefer more light can be hung near the edge of the tree. Plants growing under trees usually require more frequent watering. The good air circulation will dry the plants faster. Since the conditions tend to be harsher under a tree compared to in a greenhouse, the plants not only need to be watered more frequently but should also be fertilized regularly with a water soluble balanced fertilizer at full strength. Slotted wood baskets are the best containers to use. They allow the orchid an excellent root development and are attractive. Clay pots and plastic pots can also be used with double hangers. A well drained medium should be used. A mixture of charcoal and bark will work very well.

Plants grown under trees will be more tolerant to cold temperatures and have a higher resistance to diseases. Many times a plant which does not flower in a greenhouse will flower when placed under a tree. The shock due to the change in conditions will usually induce the plants to flower. Plants grown under trees will not look as nice and clean as plants grown in a greenhouse. However, growing under trees is very popular in South Florida. The majority of the orchids grown in this area are in small backyard green houses, under trees or a combination of both.

*Cattleya skinneri*

*Dendrobium aggregatum*

*Encyclia cordigera* var. *randii* 'Valentine'

# NUTRITION

## Feeding pattern

The frequency and strength of the fertilizer being applied depends on other conditions such as light, temperature and humidity. The stronger the light, the higher the temperature will be, resulting in higher nutritional requirements for the plants.

It is always best to water before fertilizing. The fertilizer will not be absorbed if the medium is too dry. The solution will simply flow through the medium and will not be absorbed by the medium. Mineral intake by the plant and water intake by the plant are two different mechanisms. Fertilizing plants which are wet will result in greater mineral uptake by the plants.

As a guide, fertilizing plants every two weeks in the summer or every month in the winter is usually sufficient. After applying fertilizer the next watering should a very slight watering. By not watering heavily, the fertilizer which has dried in the medium is put back into solution making it available to the plant again. In effect the plants are fertilized again. The second watering after fertilizing should be a heavy watering to flush the excess fertilizer thereby preventing a salt buildup in the medium.

## Fertilizer

An inorganic balanced water-soluble fertilizer, an 18-18-18 or 20-20-20 works best for orchids. Slow release fertilizers are not recommended since they may burn roots by releasing too much fertilizer during rainy periods.

Organic fertilizers are not recommended since most of these fertilizers must be decomposed by bacterial action before they are completely available to the plants. This requires that the fertilizer be retained in the medium until bacterial action breaks it down. If the breakdown occurs rapidly the roots may be burned. In addition the application of organic fertilizers may result in the introduction of disease organisms and organisms which increase the rate of decomposition of the medium.

Plants exhibiting a fertilizer deficiency will have yellow leaves, small growths and older leaves will fall prematurely.

Plants receiving excess fertilizer will have dark green leaves, soft growths which fall over, the tips of the leaves will burn and turn black and the pseudobulbs will begin to shrivel as a result of root burn.

Influence of pH on availability of plant nutrients (widest part indicates maximum availability)
Graph courtesy of Michigan State University

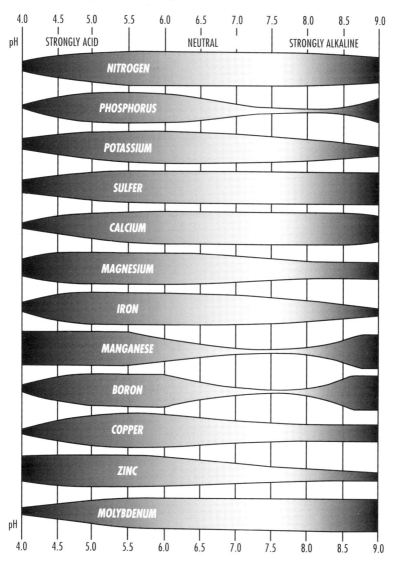

## pH Measurements

pH is a measure of how acidic or alkaline your nutrient solution or water is. The pH scale goes from 0 to 14, 7.0 is neutral, and 7 to 14 is alkaline. Generally plants prefer the pH to stay in the 5.5 to 7.5 range; beyond this certain nutrients may become less available for plants to absorb. The key is to monitor your nutrient solution on a regular basis to make sure the pH is at the right level.

# Pests and Diseases

Thrip Damage on Flowers

Bud Drop Due to Thrips

Bud Damage Due to Thrips

## Disease Prevention

A good disease prevention program is recommended and will result in stronger plants. Spraying every 21-30 days, frequency depends on weather, will successfully prevent diseases.

One of the most effective and least expensive combinations to prevent most insect infestations and both bacterial and fungal diseases is:

- Dithane - As indicated on label
- Sevin (liquid) - As indicated on label
- This combination should be used every 21-30 days.

Sevin has a low toxicity to humans and is effective against insect, slug, and snail infestations but requires at least 3 sprayings one week apart for complete control of insects. Another effective insecticide is wettable powder Orthene. Orthene usually requires two or three sprayings 10 days apart. Orthene dissolves in water making it easy to apply with a bottle applicator on the end of the hose.

Isopropyl Alcohol at 50% or 70% is excellent for spot spraying for most insect infestations. Alcohol will not damage plant tissue. It can even be used on flower buds to

Bud Damage Due to Thrips

control thrips without damage to the flowers. Alcohol will kill on contact and is not toxic to humans. Make certain that isopropyl alcohol is used not methanol or ethanol.

## Flower Thrips

Because of their small size, flower thrips are carried over large areas by wind. Flower thrips feed by piercing the leaf or petal surface and drawing sap from injured cells. Only the epidermis and relatively few meso-phyll cells are affected. On orchids, this damage is restricted to the flowers. For example, blossoms turn brown and buds open only partially. The petals, distorted with brown edges, seem to stick together.

Flower thrips are one of the most numerous and damaging insect pests of orchids. During warm periods, swarms of these tiny insects often fly in late afternoon. Their large numbers account for consider-able and rapid damage to flowers, especially those with pale petals.

Flower thrips are generally found at the base of the flower petals. They reproduce throughout the year, with the majority of their 12 to 15 generations occurring in the warmer months.

### Control

*Control of flower thrips is difficult because of constant migration from weeds, grass, flowers and trees. Old blossoms should be destroyed and applications of pesticides made at close intervals, especially in late May and June on the buds. The following pesticides give adequate control of flower thrips on a short-term basis: Orthene, Sevin, Malathion*

## Mealybugs

Female mealybugs are soft oval insects without wings. They are up to 3 mm long. Some species are covered with fluffy wax and others have long tails of fluffy wax. Male mealybugs are tiny, gnat-like insects with two wings and long tails of white wax. Mealybug

*Brown Soft Scale on Oncidium*

*Pseudobulb with Cotton Scale*

*Cotton Scale on Cattleya Leaf*

## Slugs

Fully-grown leaf which had
been attacked when young

Slug

Slugs will damage a
plant very quickly

## Roaches

Roaches eat
root-tips

Slightly hollowed-out
potato slice as bait

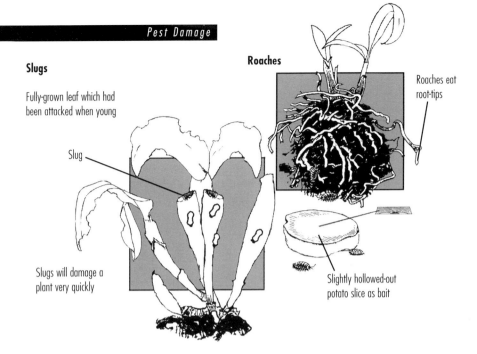

eggs are very small but are covered by a conspicuous dense, fluffy, white mass of wax. Very young nymphs are flat, oval and yellow. Older nymphs of some species are covered with fluffy, white wax.

Mealybugs are most active in warm, dry weather. Mealybugs damage plants by inserting their threadlike mouth parts into any part of the plant and sucking out sap. They excrete honeydew, a sweet, sticky liquid. Sooty molds often grow in the honeydew causing infested plants to turn black. Heavily infested plants are disfigured by the mealybugs, their ovisacs, honeydew and sooty molds. Small numbers of mealybugs are easily overlooked as they tend to wedge into crevices on plants. After the first batch of eggs hatch, the infestation becomes very noticeable. As their numbers increase, mealybugs of all sizes can be found crawling around or feeding on all surfaces of the plant.

*Control*

*Mealybugs are not easy to control. Because the eggs are enmeshed in the waxy fluff, it is difficult to get a pesticide through to kill them. If an infestation is discovered early enough, the mealybugs may be removed by a cotton swab dipped in alcohol or fingernail polish remover. Keep an eye on the plants for a few weeks to make sure no mealybugs are overlooked. If a large number of plants are infested, spray the plants thoroughly with one of the pesticide mixtures listed below. This treatment may have to be repeated two or more times at weekly intervals since new mealybugs hatch from egg masses which might have been missed by the spray.*

*Orthene, Sevin, Dursban, Malathion, Insecticidal Soap.*

### Brown Soft Scale

Living adult brown soft scale is pale yellowish-green to yellowish brown, often mottled with brown spots. Crawlers and young nymphs are yellow and almost flat in profile. Brown soft scale is cosmopolitan in tropical and subtropical regions and in greenhouses. Infestations of brown soft scale can become so heavy as to encrust the stems and petioles of their host plant. They also settle on leaves, usually along midribs and occasionally on the fruit. Colonies remove large quantities of plant fluids and can cause wilting, but they seldom kill their host. Immatures and adults produce much honeydew that serves as a medium for the growth of sooty molds. These fungi inhibit photosynthesis and make infested plants unsightly. Obnoxious insects such as ants and wasps are also attracted to feed on the honeydew.

### Control

*Brown soft scales are surprisingly difficult to control even though there is no external egg stage, and only a few very young nymphs are protected by the body of the mother at any one time. The following pesticide formulations should control brown soft scales if applied to infested plants thoroughly. A second application may be necessary. Wait about 10 days between applications. Never set a plant out in the sun to treat it. Pesticide injury may result. Keep treated plants in the shade or treat during the cooler parts of the day so the foliage will dry before the plant is exposed to direct sunlight. Orthene, Enstar, Malathion and Insecticidal Soap are effective.*

### Cotton Scale

Cottony cushion scales are rusty red with black legs and antennae. They are about 4.5mm long. The mouth parts are the piercing sucking type. The body is often obscured by wax. Cottony scale is found throughout tropical and subtropical areas. Cottony scales debilitate plants by sucking out sap. They excrete honeydew, a sweet, sticky liquid which coats infested plants. Dark fungi called sooty molds grow in the honeydew. Heavily infested plants become chlorotic but darkened. Leaves drop prematurely, and heavily infested plants may die during periods of stress.

### Control

*Because the cottony cushion scale is an introduced pest, it has few predators and parasites. The following insecticides are suitable for use on orchids: Orthene, Sevin, Dursban. The use of a spreader-sticker is recommended for cottony scale control to aid in the penetration of the pesticide into the ovisac and through the wax covering the scales.*

### Spider Mites (Red Spider)

Spider mites are small (about 0.3 mm) flat and orange to red with black spots. Several species of spider mites feed on a variety of orchids. The phalaenopsis mite (*Tenuipalpus pacificus*) and the oncidium mite (*Brevipalpus oncidii*) are fairly specific for orchids. Another spider mite, *Tenuipalpus orchidarum*, also feeds on orchids. With their needle-sharp mouth parts, spider mites puncture the epidermis of the host plant and suck out the juices. This causes a pale spot which may later turn brown. Infested plants slowly turn reddish-brown.

### Control

*Several pesticides are labeled for "mite" control. Most spider mites feed on the lower leaf surface so that the pesticide spray must be directed upwards to contact the mites. The following pesticides are suitable for home use: Avid, Talstar, Dursban and Kelthane.*

### Caterpillars

There are several thousand kinds of moths and butterflies in Florida which lay eggs from which hatch destructive caterpillars that feed on orchids. The moths and butterflies (adults) cannot do any damage to plants themselves; only the caterpillars damage the plants.

*Spider Mites on Cattleya Leaf*

*Spider Mites on Oncidium Leaf*

### Control

The single attack of a leaf-feeding insect will seldom kill a healthy plant. Repeated defoliations, however, may weaken and make them susceptible to destruction by other insects, diseases, severe cold weather, drought, etc. The following pesticides are labeled for caterpillars: Orthene, Talstar, Mavrik.

## Roaches

Roaches hide in pots, coming out at night to eat flowers and root tips. They can cause serious damage by eating root tips. Orchids will usually produce roots only once a year, if the tips are eaten the plants can become seriously dehydrated.

### Control

Roaches are difficult to control because they must eat a large amount of plant material before they ingest enough insecticide to kill them. Harris roach tablets are an excellent control. They are attracted to the tablets and usually will not eat any of the plant after they eat the tablet. Orthene will also control roaches.

### Slugs and Snails

Slugs and snails are soft, slimy, slender animals more closely related to clams than insects. They have stalked eyes and two small feelers. Some species grow to 3 or more inches long. Eggs are oval and up to 3 mm long. They are clear, cream or yellow and are usually laid in masses sometimes in a gelatin like substance. Slugs and snails are found throughout the United States and Europe. They feed on the leaves and flowers. They are most damaging to tender, young growths and flowers in spring. Damage on foliage usually appears between the veins and on leaf margins. Small slugs and snails rasp away the leaf or petal surface. Large slugs and snails consume whole leaves, petals and sometimes entire plants if the plants are small, A silvery slime trail is left behind. They are active at night and during cloudy, warm weather. During bright warm weather, they usually hide under boards, stones, debris or tunnel into the soil.

## Control

Sanitation - Populations can be reduced by eliminating their breeding and hiding places. Remove rotting boards, logs, pots and other debris from the area. Compost or destroy plant refuse and properly stack or store flats, boxes, etc., which provide shelter for slugs. Trim tall grass and weeds along fences and ditches in the vicinity of the plants.

Traps - Boards or other flat objects on the soil. These traps should be at least 6" by 6". Each morning remove the slugs from beneath the traps and destroy them.

Pesticides - A molluscicide (slug-killing agent) can be applied in walkways. For best control, apply the molluscicide on a warm, clear night under boards or traps. Two or more treatments at 5 to 7 day intervals may be necessary to obtain adequate control. In the list below are pesticide formulations labeled for slug and snail control.

- carbaryl (Sevin) 5%
- metaldehyde 2 to 3.3%
- calcium arsenate 5% + metaldehyde 2%
- carbaryl (Sevin) 4 to 5% + metaldehyde 1 to 3.25%

Snails

Snail Damage on Cattleya Flower

## Orchid Diseases and Treatment

| PESTS | SYMPTOMS | TREATMENT |
|---|---|---|
| Flower Thrips | Buds turn brown or drop | Orthene, Sevin |
| Mealybugs | Disfigures plants | Orthene, Sevin |
| Brown Soft Scales | Disfigures plants | Orthene, Malathion |
| Cotton Scales | Disfigures plants | Orthene, Sevin |
| Caterpillars | Eat parts of plants | Orthene, Talstar |
| Roaches | Chew flowers, stunt plant growth | Harris Roach Tablets, Orthene |

### Bacterial and Fungal Diseases

| | | |
|---|---|---|
| Black Rot | New growth soft black | Remove black area – Captan or Dithane |
| Leaf Spot (Cercospora) | Black or yellow spots | Remove leaf – Captan or Dithane |
| Bacterial Rots | Clear spots | Remove area – Captan or Dithane |
| Crown Rot | Apical leaf dies | Remove leaf – Hydrogen Peroxide |
| Viral Diseases | Flower color break Black streaks on leaves | Prevention of spread – sterilize tools |

## English and Metric-System Equivalents

1 inch = 25.4 millimeters

1 foot = 30.48 centimeters

1 yard = 91.44 centimeters

1 mile = 1.609 kilometers

1 gallon = 3.785 liters

1 ounce = 28.35 grams

1 pound = 453.6 grams

1 millimeter = 0.03937 inches

1 centimeter = 0.3937 inches

1 meter = 39.37 inches

1 kilometer = 0.62137 miles

1 liter = 1.057 quarts

1 gram = 15.43 grains

1 kilograms = 2.205 pounds

## Appropriate Conversion Factors and Relationships Among Units of Measure

### Liquid Measure

1 ounce (fluid) = 2 Tbs. = 6 tsp. = 1.805 cu. in. = 29.54 ml

1 teaspoon = 50-60 drops = 0.33 Tbs. = 0.167 oz. = 0.301 cu. in. = 14.79 ml

1 tablespoon = 3 tsp. = 0.5 oz. = 0.0625 cup = 0.9025 cu. in. = 14.79 ml

1 cup = 16 Tbs. = 8 oz. = 0.5 pt. = 0.25 qt. = 14.44 cu. in. = 236.32 ml

1 pint = 32 Tbs. = 16 oz. = 2 cups = 0.5 qt. = 28.88 cu. in. = 472.65 ml

1 quart = 64 Tbs. = 32 oz. = 4 cups = 0.25 gal. = 57.76 cu. in. = 946 ml

1 gallon = 4 qt. = 8 pt. = 16 cups = 128 oz. = 231 cu. in. = 3.785 liter

1 milliliter = 1 cu. cm. = 0.001 liter = 0.203 tsp.

1 liter = 1000 cu. cm = 1.057 qt. = 0.2642 gal. = 61.02 cu. in.

## Per-Gallon Equivalents for Diluting Concentrated Fertilizers and Chemicals

*Some commercial products give dilution rates per 100 gal. (380 liters). Listed below are the approximate equivalents for 1 gal. (3.8 liters)*

### Liquids

2 gal./100 gal. = 5 Tbs./gal.

1 gal./100 gal. = 7.5 tsp./gal.

2 qt./100 gal. = 3.75 tsp./gal.

1 qt./100 gal. = 2 tsp/gal.

1 pt./100 gal. = 1 tsp/gal.

8 oz./100 gal. = 0.5 tsp./gal.

4 oz./100 gal. = 0.25 tsp./gal.

### Solids

5 lb./100 gal. = 4.75 tsp./gal.

4 lb./100 gal. = 3.75 tsp./gal.

2 lb./100 gal. = 2 tsp./gal.

1 lb./100 gal. = 1 tsp./gal.

8 oz./100 gal. = 0.5 tsp./gal.

### Dilutions

For some chemicals, dilution rates are given as a ratio. The following are approximate equivalent rates for a single gallon.

| | | | | | |
|---|---|---|---|---|---|
| 1:100 | = | 2 Tbs. + 2 tsp./gal. | = | 10.0 ml/l |
| 1:200 | = | 4 tsp./gal. | = | 5.2 ml/l |
| 1:400 | = | 2 tsp./gal. | = | 2.6 ml/l |
| 1:800 | = | 1 tsp./gal. | = | 1.3 ml/l |
| 1:1000 | = | 3/4 tsp./gal. | = | 1.0 ml/l |
| 1:2000 | = | 3/8 tsp./gal. | = | 0.5 ml/l |

*For some chemicals, dilution rate are given as parts per million (ppm). The following are approximate equivalents.*

| % sol.* | dilution | ppm• | tsp./gal. | | | ml/l |
|---|---|---|---|---|---|---|
| 0.001 | 1:100,000 | 10 | 0.00768 | or | 3/4 tsp./100 gal. | 0.01 |
| 0.005 | 1:50,000 | 20 | 0.0154 | or | 3/4 tsp./50 gal. | 0.02 |
| 0.01 | 1:10,000 | 100 | 0.0768 | or | 3/4 tsp./10 gal. | 0.1 |
| 0.02 | 1:5,000 | 200 | 0.1536 | or | 3/4 tsp./5 gal. | 0.2 |
| 0.05 | 1:2,000 | 500 | 0.384 | or | 3/8 tsp./ gal. | 0.5 |
| 0.10 | 1:1,000 | 1000 | 0.768 | or | 3/4 tsp./gal. | 1.0 |
| 1.0 | 1:100 | 10,000 | 7.68 | or | 7 2/3 tsp./gal. | 10.0 |

\* This assumes an initial concentration of 100%. To use with different concentrations, divide 100 by the % of concentration and multiply the tsp./gal. or ml/l by the answer. For example, when using a fertilizer containing 20% nitrogen, divide 100 by 20, which yields 5. Then multiply 5 by the amount shown under tsp./gal. or ml/l.

• If a solution of 100 ppm is desired when using a 20% concentration, multiply 0.0768 tsp./gal. or 0.1 ml/l by 5. In other words, it requires 0.0768 tsp./gal. or 0.1 ml/l of 100% concentrate to give a solution with 100 ppm; but it takes 5 times these amounts of 20% concentrate to produce a mixture with the same strength.

---

## Appropriate Conversion Factors and Relationships Among Units of Measure

### Dry Measure

1 teaspoon = 0.33 Tbs.     1 quart = 2 pt.

1 tablespoon = 3 tsp.     1 gallon = 4 qt.

1 cup = 16 Tbs. = 48 tsp.   1 peck = 2 gal.

1 pint = 2 cups

### Weight

1 ounce = 0.0625 lb. = 28.35 g = 3 Tbs. (dry) = 2 Tbs. (liquid)

1 pound = 16 oz. = 453.6 g = 2 cups

1 gram = 15.43 grains = 0.0353 oz. = 0.1058 Tbs. = 0.3175 tsp.

1 kilogram = 1000 g = 2.205 lb. = 35.28 oz.

### Abbreviations

| | | |
|---|---|---|
| BTU | = | British thermal unit |
| CFM | = | cubic feet per minute |
| cu. | = | cubic |
| ft. | = | feet |
| gal. | = | gallon |
| in. | = | inch |
| lb. | = | pound |
| oz. | = | ounce |
| pt. | = | pint |
| qt. | = | quart |
| sec. | = | second |
| sq. | = | square |
| Tbs. | = | tablespoon |
| tsp. | = | teaspoon |
| yd. | = | yard |
| cm | = | centimeter |
| g | = | gram |
| kg | = | kilogram |
| l | = | liter |
| l/sec. | = | liters per second |
| m | = | meter |
| ml | = | milliliter |
| mm | = | millimeter |

# BACTERIAL AND FUNGAL DISEASES

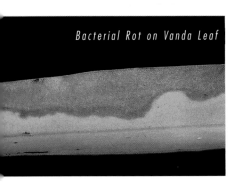

*Bacterial Rot on Vanda Leaf*

*Cercospora on Cattleya Leaf*

*Black Rot on Cattleya New Growth*

## Black Rot

Black rot usually infects young immature growths of cattleya or young pseudobulbs and leaves. This disease spreads rapidly from plant to plant, therefore must be contained immediately. It usually occurs during periods of very high humidity or excessive rain. Affected areas become soft and black. An entire plant will be killed in a short time.

### Control

*The affected area must be removed, making sure to cut well below the blackened tissue. The plant and all adjacent plants must be sprayed. Captan or Dithane are effective in controlling this disease.*

## Leaf Spot (*Cercospora*)

Leaf spot appears as a yellow to black irregular spot on leaves. The affected area remains hard. Although this disease will not kill a plant it will cover most of the leaves and make a plant very unsightly. This disease spreads rapidly and must be controlled quickly.

### Control

*The affected area must be removed and the plant and adjacent plants must be sprayed. Captan or Dithane will effectively control this disease.*

## Bacterial Rots

Bacteria infect many different orchids. Cattleyas and dendrobiums are susceptible mainly on the new growths which quickly become discolored and soft almost appearing to melt away. Vandas get a bacterial rot which starts at the base of the plant causing the leaves to fall off rapidly until the plant is dead. In addition, a form of crown rot is also due to bacteria in vandaceous plants and quickly kills the plant. Phalaenopsis are extremely susceptible to bacterial spotting. Spots appear on the leaves which quickly turn almost clear and soft.

### Control

*These bacterial rots are very difficult to control. In all cases the affected area must be removed and strong bactericide used. Captan and Dithane can be* used effectively after the affected area is removed. Good air circulation and a good preventive spray program are the best tools to prevent the disease.

## Crown Rot (Monopodial Orchids)

Vandaceous plants (monopodial) will on occasion have the apical growth attacked by a fungus. It is first detected when the apical leaf (last leaf) turns black. This disease not only travels rapidly in the affected plant but will spread to other plants. Appropriate action must be taken quickly.

### Control

*The apical leaf should be pulled out and the apex of the plant treated. Hydrogen peroxide full strength can be applied to the crown. Afterwards the plant and adjacent plants should be sprayed with Captan or Dithane.*

## Viral Diseases

Viral diseases invade the cellular parts of the plant and are impossible to kill without killing the host plant. There are several different species of viruses which infect orchids. All initially reduce the vigor of the plant but in most cases the plants eventually overcome the effects of the virus. Viruses will cause yellow streaking on the leaves, black and white necrotic areas on the leaves, streaks of light green or purple on the leaves or irregular black rings on the underside of the leaf. Cattleya color break virus will cause color streaks on all of the flowers.

Vanda Crown Rot

Cattleya Color Break Virus

### Control

*The only protection against viruses is to prevent their spread. Viruses are only spread by mechanical means. If all tools are sterilized between cuts the viruses will not be spread. Whether to destroy plants which are infected is a personal choice. Many of the older hybrids are infested with viruses. As long as care is taken between cuts it is safe to keep the plants in a collection. Plants with cattleya color break virus should be destroyed because it disfigures the flowers.*

*Tools used to cut should be sterilized by baking for 1/2 hour at 500° F; autoclaving at 15 lbs of pressure for 15 minutes or using a sterilizing solution. A solution of 2% formaldehyde and 2% sodium hydroxide, 10% aqueous solution of trisodium orthophosphate or 50% Physan or RD-20 will effectively sterilize the tools.*

Virus Symptoms on Cattleya Leaf

# CONTAINERS

**Clay Pot**

## Pots
- Shallow clay pots with slits on side are best for proper drainage
- Plastic pots – inexpensive – long lasting – can fall over with weight of flowers
- Plastic net pot – excellent air circulation for roots

## Cleaning pots - clay or plastic
- Bleach solution 25-30% overnight to remove algae
- Muriatic acid to remove salts – do not mix with bleach.

**Wire Basket**

## Baskets
- Wood slats – teak, cypress, cedar, redwood
- Last 3-5 years
- Prevent algal growth by spraying with Captan or an algicide every 3-4 months
- Fill with chunk tree fern, sphagnum moss, charcoal or charcoal/bark mix
- Do not use screen lining – decreases air circulation

## Tree Fern Baskets
- Cut with grain, drains fast – good for cattleyas
- Cut against grain, holds water – good for phalaenopsis
- Use according to water requirements of plant

**Wood Basket**

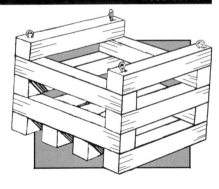

## Wire Baskets
- Inexpensive – long lasting
- Fill with tree fern chunks, coconut husk chunks, charcoal or sphagnum moss

## Approximate Pot Volumes

Pot volumes vary dramatically depending on pot shape. These volumes may be used to approximate the amount of medium needed or to estimate the quantity of a supplement that is appropriate for small to medium-sized pot.

### Round Azalea Pots (height = ³/₄ diameter of top)

4 in. (10 cm) = 1 ½ cups (354 ml)
5 in. (13 cm) = 3 ⅝ cups (857 ml)
6 in. (15 cm) = 5 ½ cups (1300 ml)
7 in. (18 cm) = 8 cups (1890 ml)

### Round Bulb Pans (height = ¹/₂ diameter of top)

5 in. (13 cm) = 2 ¾ cups (473 ml)
6.5 in. (17 cm) = 5 ¾ cups (1359 ml)

8 in. (20 cm) = 8 cups (1890 ml)

### Round Standard Pots (height = ³/₄ diameter of top)

1.5 in. (4 cm) = ⅛ cups (29.5 ml)
2 in. (5 cm) = ¼ cups (59 ml)
2.5 in. (6 cm) = ⅜ cups (89 ml)
3 in. (8 cm) = ¾ cups (178 ml)
3.5 in. (9 cm) = 1 ¼ cups (295 ml)
4 in. (10 cm) = 1 ⅞ cups (443 ml)
5 in. (13 cm) = 3 ¾ cups (886 ml)
6 in. (15 cm) = 6 ½ cups (1536 ml)

## Tree Fern and Cork Slab

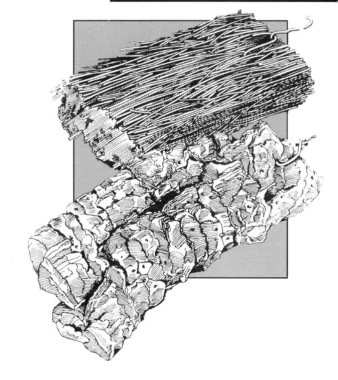

# POTTING MEDIA

Each grower must find the right medium for his conditions and should not change the medium unless there is a problem. All of the culture elements (light, water, temperature, aeration and nutrition) must be adjusted to the medium. Some media will hold more moisture than others and watering must be adjusted accordingly. Also some media contains nutrients which are released as it deteriorates and fertilizing must be adjusted.

*Osmunda Fiber*

## Osmunda fiber
- One of the oldest known media
- Roots of the osmunda fern – found in swampy areas
- Gives plants a good balance of nutrients
- Heavy fertilizing not necessary
- Difficult to use properly – must be packed very tight and the grain must be oriented to give good drainage
- May have to be washed to remove salts
- Expensive and difficult to find
- Good for all genera

## Tree fern fiber
- Root of tree fern that forms around the trunk
- Most tree ferns are endangered species or threatened

*Tree Fern*

- Many different species - Mexico, Guatemala, South America
- Low in nutrients - must be fertilized regularly
- Acid - pH 5 - 6 - excellent for most epiphytes
- Snow mold common problem

*Fir Bark*

## Fir (Redwood) bark
- Bark nuggets – 1/4" - 1/2"
- Bark broken up, tumbled and dried
- Decays rapidly – lasts for 1 - 2 years
- Charcoal can be added to retard decay – lasts for 3 - 4 years
- Excellent for phalaenopsis, cattleyas, dendrobiums

## Solite - Alliflor - Gravelite
- These are all names for expanded clay – used by concrete industry to make light-weight blocks
- Neutral pH – No nutritional value
- Good drainage
- No deterioration but salts may accumulate - frequent flushing required

Expanded Clay

Sphagnum Moss

## Charcoal
- Neutral medium
- Excellent drainage – very slow deterioration
- A good medium to use for general culture especially when mixed with other materials
- Use large chunks for vandas, medium for cattleyas, phalaenopsis and dendrobiums and fine for seedlings
- No noticeable salt build-up – good for 5-6 years

## Mixed media
- Tree fern and redwood chips
- Excellent acid medium for cattleyas, dendrobiums and oncidiums
- Mix 3/4 tree fern with 1/4 redwood chips

## Bark and charcoal
- Easy to use, inexpensive
- Excellent for cattleyas, dendrobiums, phalaenopsis, oncidiums and seedlings
- Mix according to amount of moisture retention required
  - 100 to 70% bark for phalaenopsis
  - 20% bark for vandas
  - 50% for most other genera

Charcoal

## Coconut husk
- Chunks excellent for vandas, phalaenopsis and dendrobiums
- Best used in baskets with good drainage
- Fiber used also for mature plants

## Sphagnum moss
- Slow deterioration
- Holds water for a long time – less watering
- Excellent for cattleya and phalaenopsis seedlings and mature phalaenopsis
- Light weight - plants in flower can become top heavy and tip over
- Many different qualities: New Zealand (Chile), Florida and Wisconsin

Coconut Husk

## Filler for bottom of pot
- Used to improve drainage
- Broken pots
  - If pieces too large they will harbor roaches and snails
- Styrofoam peanuts or chunks
  - Will not deteriorate, dries quickly - remains cool

# Propagation of Orchids – Asexual

## Dividing and Repotting Plants

### Sympodial Orchids

Sympodial orchids like cattleyas, dendrobiums and oncidiums are divided into divisions of 3 bulbs or more. When the decision is made where to divide the plant the rhizome is cut and the division is cleaned of all dry material. Usually the roots are trimmed. All dead roots are trimmed off and the good roots are usually trimmed down to a few inches long. Plants should only be repotted when new roots appear on the newest growth. By doing this the new roots will come out and the plant will establish itself very quickly.

The back bulbs which remain after the front leads are cut off will usually die if not treated correctly. They can be potted, watered and then placed in a clear plastic bag that is sealed and placed in a shady place. Usually after a few weeks new growth will appear and then new roots. When the new growth matures and the plant has rooted then it can be removed from the plastic bag.

Many plants develop keikis which are small vegetative growths originating from meristematic buds on nodes of canes or flower spikes. Dendrobiums will naturally form keikis on old canes. If they develop on new canes instead of flowers this means that the plants were overwatered or not given sufficient sunlight. Old canes of dendrobiums can be cut off and placed on damp sphagnum moss. This will cause keikis to develop on the nodes. Epidendrums, especially reed-stem types, will commonly develop keikis from the nodes on the flower spikes. Old spikes of phaius can be cut off immediately after flowering and if kept moist will develop keikis on the nodes. Keikis should be removed and potted when they have approximately three roots as long as the vegetative growth.

The tools used for cutting the plants should always be sterilized between cuts. This includes cutting off flowers. Sterilizing the tools will prevent the spread of viral diseases.

### Monopodial Orchids

Monopodial orchids like vandas are divided by making top cuttings or removing basal keikis. A top cutting should always have 2-3 roots. If possible leaves should be left on the bottom part. If the bottom part has leaves, keikis will develop. Bare bottom stems will usually die and do not produce keikis. Keikis which develop at the base of the plants should be left on the plant until they flower. If removed too early the keikis will take a long time to flower. Once they have flowered on the original plant they will continue to do so after they are removed.

Phalaenopsis usually do not grow tall enough to make top cuttings. These are usually repotted after they flower. Care should be taken not to remove any live roots. Additionally, phalaenopsis will produce keikis on the flower spikes. These keikis can be removed and planted after they have developed 2-3 roots.

### Attaching Orchids to Slabs

A popular way to grow orchids,

especially species, is on slabs or driftwood. The most common slab materials are tree fern and cork. Driftwood is also used and can be used to produce works of art.

Tree fern slabs can vary in quality. The grain can be loose or very tightly packed. The loosely packed slabs will dry faster and the slabs with the tight grain will retain moisture longer. Additionally, how the grain runs on the slab will also determine how much moisture will be retained by the slab. If the grain runs from the top of the slab to the bottom it will dry faster, if the grain is perpendicular to the face of the slab it will dry very slowly. The amount of moisture that the slab retains can be used to determine which orchids to attach to the slab. Plants which require more moisture can be planted on tight grained slabs with the grain perpendicular to the face of the slab. The other slabs can be used for plants which like to dry out rapidly. A tie wire of 16 gauge can be used to attach the plant to the slab and to make a hanger on the slab. Tree fern has recently become very expensive and difficult to purchase. Snow mold can be a problem on tree fern. The white mold can cover the roots and suffocate the plant. Frequent spray with a good fungicide is recommended.

Cork is commonly used as slab material. Cork deteriorates slowly and does not hold much moisture. It is excellent for plants that grow in dry conditions. For plants that prefer more moisture some sphagnum moss can be added around the roots. A tie wire of 16 gauge can be used to attach the plants and to make a hanger. Due to the nature of the cork it must be drilled to pass the wire through. Cork has a tendency to grow algae. The algae can suffocate the roots and eventually cause the death of the plant. A good fungicide-algacide must be used regularly.

Driftwood is becoming more difficult to obtain and expensive. If the driftwood comes from salt water it must be leached for several months or most plants will not attach. Due to the beautiful nature of driftwood it can be used to make very interesting plantings.

# PROPAGATION OF ORCHIDS – SEXUAL

Pscyhilis Seed Pod

Sexual propagation of orchids is either by "selfing", self-fertilization, which transfers the pollinia from the anther to the stigma of the same flower or by cross-fertilization, crosses of two different individuals.

## Pollination

Pollination is the transferring of pollinia from the anther to the stigma. This can occur naturally by bees, flies, birds, butterflies, moths, wasps or mosquitoes. In nature pollinators visit the flowers to feed or by deceptive mimicry.

## Seed Pod

After pollination the sepals, petals and lip fold within 1-3 days and the ovary begins to enlarge. Enlargement continues until the pod matures. Ovules are not present in the mature flower. Ovule development is initiated by pollination. Ovules take from 8 to 150 days to develop. The interval between pollination and fertilization is 8 to 150 days. Usually immediately after ovule development fertilization occurs. However, complete seed pod development takes longer.

Phalaenopsis Seed Pod

Epidendrum Seed Pod

Cattleya Seed Pod

# CROSSABILITY – INTERGENERIC HYBRIDS

In orchids the genetic ability to produce hybrids at both the species level and the generic level is very high. The orchids are a newly evolved group therefore, the species and genera are more genetically similar. Genetic incompatibilities have not had as long to evolve. In addition, orchid seeds do not contain endosperm. Endosperm is 3N tissue, the production of this tissue during seed development adds to sterility.

Epiphytic orchids have the highest degree of crossability, not only because they have evolved more recently, but because the epiphytic habitat is an unstable habitat that leads to more genetic variability. Plants in the epiphytic habitat have less competition for space therefore more speciation occurs resulting in more closely related species and genera.

Terrestrial orchids demonstrate less crossability. Evolutionally they are an older group and are genetically more stable. This genetic stability is added to by the fact that the terrestrial habitat is more stable than the epiphytic habitat.

Intergeneric hybrids are much more common in epiphytic orchids than in terrestrial orchids.

Renanthopsis Firey Gem

Wils. Michoacan

Oda. Golden Rialto X Oda. Ingera

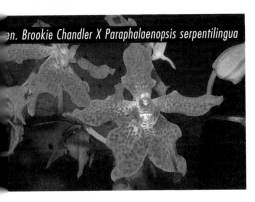
en. Brookie Chandler X Paraphalaenopsis serpentilingua

# CLASSIFICATION

## Species

Species are naturally occurring populations of plants with similar characteristics which share a common gene pool (individuals interbreed) and are reproductively isolated (limited gene flow) from other populations (species).

Family . . . . . . . . . . . Orchidaceae
Subfamily . . . . . . . . Epidendroideae
Tribe . . . . . . . . . . . . Epidendreae
Subtribe . . . . . . . . . Laeliinae
Genus . . . . . . . . . . . *Anacheilium*
Species . . . . . . . . . . *cochleatum*
Variety (Subspecies) . . *triandrum*
Forma . . . . . . . . . . . *alba*
Clonal Variety . . . . . . 'RIO'

*Anacheilium cochleatum* var. *triandrum alba* 'RIO'

The generic name is always capitalized.

Species name and other lower taxa are always written in lower case.

All taxa are written in italics or underlined.

The name of a species is not properly written unless the author citation is included, however in most informal orchid literature the author citation is not included.

*Epidendrum fehlingii* Sauleda. This indicates that the species *fehlingii* was first described by Sauleda as a new species in the genus *Epidendrum*.

*Encyclia fehlingii* (Sauleda) Sauleda & Adams. This indicates that the species *fehlingii* was transferred by Sauleda and Adams to the genus *Encyclia*.

## Hybrids

Hybrids can be primary hybrids, a cross of two species, or intergeneric hybrids, a cross involving two or more genera. Intergeneric hybrids can also be primary or complex hybrids.

Primary hybrid – cross of two species: C. Rubencito (*C. aurantiaca* X *C. dowiana*)

Intergeneric hybrid – a cross involving two or more genera can be a primary or complex hybrid:

Epicattleya Epiorange (*C. aurantiaca* X *Epidendrum alatum*)

Complex hybrid – cross of a species and a hybrid or two hybrids

Hybrid name – Blc. Mem. Crispin Rosales 'Mindi' HCC/AOS, AM/AOS, SM/SFOS

Parentage – (Lc. Bonanza X Blc. Norman's Bay) Parent which carried the seed pod is written first

Clonal Variety – 'Mindi'

Awards - HCC/AOS, AM/AOS, SM/SFOS

Blc. Mem. Crispin Rosales 'Mindi' SM/SFOS, HCC/AOS, AM/AOS (Lc. Bonanza 'Tradewinds' AM/AOS X Blc. Norman's Bay 'Gothic' FCC/RHS)

## Naming Hybrids

Hybrids are named through a registration authority. The authority is The Royal Horticultural Society, Vincent Square, London, SW1P 2PE, England

A hybridizer may name a hybrid after the hybrid has flowered, if it has not been previously named.

Application forms can be obtained from RHS. Persons other than the hybridizer may name a hybrid with the written permission of hybridizer.

# Green Pod Culture

The green pod method of sowing orchid seed is the most common method used.

## Harvesting Times for Seed Capsules

Cattleya Hybrids

| | |
|---|---|
| Labiata type, white, lavender, white with purple lip | 5 to 6 months |
| Bifoliate | 4 to 5 months |
| Slc., Pot., yellow cattleyas | 5 months |
| Epicattleya, Cattleytonia and other novelties | 4 to 5 months |
| *Epidendrum* or *Encyclia* hybrids | 4 to 5 months |
| *Epidendrum pseudoepidendrum* or any reed stem epidendrums | 90 days |
| *Brassavola nodosa* and other terete *Brassavola* hybrids | 4 to 5 months |
| *Rhyncholaelia (Brassavola) digbyana* and *R. glauca* hybrids | 5 to 6 months |
| *Laelia* and *Schomburgkia* hybrids | 4 to 5 months |
| *Broughtonia* hybrids | 60 to 90 days |

Mule Ear and related oncidiums

| | |
|---|---|
| *Oncidium luridum, O. splendidum, O. lanceanum* | 6 to 8 months |
| Miniature (Equitant) *Oncidium* hybrids (*Tolumnia*) | 60 days |
| *Oncidium triquetrum* | 5 months |
| *Oncidium sphacelatum* and related *Oncidium* hybrids | 4 months |
| *Oncidium papilio, O. kramerianum* and *O. limminghei* hybrids | 100 days |
| *Miltonia* and *Odontoglossum* hybrids | 4 months |
| *Vanda, Ascocentrum* and Ascocenda hybrids | 5 to 7 months |

After 65 days *Vanda* and Ascocenda seed capsules may turn slightly yellow but are NOT ready to be planted and should be allowed to remain on the plant the full length of time. If the capsule does not contain viable seed it will usually continue to turn yellow and drop off.

| | | |
|---|---|---|
| *Rhynchostylis* hybrids | | 5 to 8 months |
| *Phalaenopsis* hybrids | large flowered | 120 to 150 days |
| | small flowered - novelty | 150 to 190 days |
| *Dendrobium* hybrids | | |
| *Dendrobium phalaenopsis* hybrids | | 4 to 5 months |
| *Dendrobium nobile* hybrids | | 5 months |
| *Dendrobium pierardii* and other pendulous hybrids | | 6 to 7 months |
| Antelope *Dendrobium* hybrids | | 4 to 5 months |

The above mentioned time intervals refer to THE PLANT CARRYING THE SEED CAPSULE; usually the pollen parent does not influence the time interval.

Ex.: *O. papilio* X *O. luridum* requires 100 days. *O. luridum* X *O. papilio* requires 7 months

Time required for complex intergeneric hybrids sometimes is only established after the capsule splits. Safeguard against splitting by making 2 or more seed capsules of same cross – after first capsule splits, harvest the remaining pods. The longer a seed capsule is allowed to remain on the plant without danger of losing the plant or the seed capsule, the better the results obtained.

# Seed Germination

Working in Laminar Flow Hood

Replating Seedlings

Flasks Inside Laminar Hood

## Symbiotic

Orchid seed is very tiny, hundreds of thousands to millions of seed are produced in a pod. The seed has no endosperm, only a dry outer coat for wind and water distribution and an undifferentiated embryo called a proembryo. Large numbers of seeds are produced because of the low survival rate in nature. Since the seeds have no nutrient reserve, they must find the proper conditions for germination in a very short time. The basal cells in the proembryo contain a substance which attracts fungal hyphae. The hyphae of the proper fungus penetrates the basal cells and produces storage hyphae. These storage hyphae undergo digestion releasing the nutrients that the proembryo needs for germination. The large numbers of seeds are produced because the chances of a seed finding the proper conditions with the fungus present are almost none.

## Asymbiotic

In the lab the seeds can be germinated independently from the root fungus. An artificial growing medium can be used which contains all of the nutrients which the seeds require. This medium however, has a large amount of sugar and therefore, must be placed in a sealed container and sterilized. This sterile medium then can only be used in a sterile transfer case.

### Preparation of Medium

The nutrients which include agar and large amounts of sugar are weighed and then dissolved in warm water. The nutrient solution is poured into flasks which are sterilized in an autoclave at 15 lbs. of pressure for 15 minutes.

### Transfer Case

The sowing of the seed and subsequent transplants are done in a sterile transfer case. The transfer case can be an airtight plastic case with gloves attached to rings to work with in the case or a forced air case called a laminar flow hood. A sterilizing solution usually made from commercial bleach is used to sterilize all of the flasks, tools and the inside of the transfer case.

### Seed Sowing

While the transfer case is being sterilized, the seed pods from which the seeds are going to be sown are placed in a sterilizing solution. The seed inside the case is sterile but the outside of the pod must be sterilized. Usually after thirty minutes the pod is sterile and it can be cut open and the seed carefully removed and spread on the agar. The seed will germinate in 1-3 months.

### Replating

After the seeds germinate they must be transplanted into another flask. When the seed germinates it is too thick and will die from lack of nutrients. To transplant the seedlings the original seed flask must be placed back into a sterile transfer case and the seedlings are transplanted into a new flasks. After 6-8 months the seedlings will be ready to be removed from the flasks.

Laminar Flow Hood

Lab Apparatus

Replated Flasks

# Storing Flasks and Removing Seedlings from Flasks

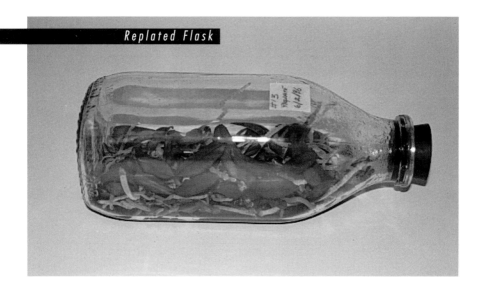

Replated Flask

The flasks must remain sealed or contamination will occur.

- Store under low light intensity
- 80-90% shade screening
- Fiberglass cover
- In a window
- 75-80° F optimal
- Extremes tolerated for short time (30-110° F)
- No direct water - low humidity

**Removing Plants From Flask**

Carefully break flask or remove plants roots first with tweezers or a wire hook.

Wash plants with plain water to remove all agar.

Leave clumps together and plant as one - can be separated later - smaller plants will usually die if separated from clump.

Pot large plants individually in 2 or 3" pots - pot smaller plants in a community pot or in a tray.

Water plants thoroughly after planting to clean medium.

Spray with a fungicide/bactericide – Physan or Dithane.

Resume normal watering and fertilizing.

Repeat spraying with fungicide/bactericide every 3-4 weeks.

# POTTING

When potting seedlings from the flask, use a 5" plastic bulb pan. The pots are soaked in a mild Physan sterilization solution prior to use. The potting medium consists of 5 parts tree fern, 10 parts fir bark, 10 parts charcoal and 3 parts Aliflor. Add 1 part sphagnum moss to the aforementioned mix (all of the ingredients are fine grade size). In the event fine grade tree fern is not available, fine grade Aliflor may be substituted. Potting medium is soaked in a solution of Physan, 20-20-20 fertilizer and SUPERthrive.

One-quarter of the pot bottom is filled with charcoal. The medium is then poured into the pot to 1/2" from the rim. The seedlings are removed from the flasks and the roots are separated from the medium with a pair of 12" forceps. The seedlings are graded by size and then placed in the same solution that is used for the potting mix. They are soaked for about 5 minutes. The pots are placed in a plastic dishpan in an elevated position about 2" below the rim of the dishpan. (Brick pavers are used to set the pot on to achieve proper elevation.) Water is then poured into the dishpan to about level with the pot rim. This causes the medium to become soupy and the small plantlets can be inserted, utilizing a small spatula, with a minimum of effort. When the community pot is full, it is lifted from the dishpan and the gravital pull of the water draining from the pot seats the plant roots into the medium.

## Care for Community Pot Seedlings

Seedlings in community pots require considerably less light than established mature plants. About 500 to 800 foot candles, or 90 percent shade. Plants require daily misting with a fine spray of water, keeping the community pots slightly on the moist side during the heat of the day. When the small plants begin to root, a normal regimen of watering and fertilizing can be started. The plants remain in the community pots for about eight months to one year before being transplanted.

## Potting Community Pot Seedlings

When community pot plants are ready for transplanting, they are moved to 2 1/2" and 3" plastic pots. An occasional plant will be large enough to be placed in a 4" pot. The young plants are removed from the community pots and sprayed with the same solution of Physan, fertilizer and SUPERthrive used for soaking the community pot plants. One-quarter of each pot is filled with fine grade pumice stone for drainage. A small amount of the potting mix is placed over the drainage material. The plant is placed in the center of the pot and mix is filled in around it. The mix is the same composition used for community pots. Some of the seedlings may be a bit tall and will not stand upright in the pot. A small clip on the stake made out of #17 gauge wire is used to hold the plant in place. By looping the top of the fine wire stake around the seedling it gives the plant adequate support. Do not forget to place proper identification labels in the pots.

## Post Potting Care for Community Pot Seedlings

At this point in the growth cycle the small seedlings require higher light levels than the community pots. Increase the light level to about 1,200 foot candles. The plants are misted daily to avoid dehydration and normal watering and fertilizing are resumed as roots begin to show. The plants remain in small individual pots on an average of about one year before being transplanted.

## Potting Process for Near Blooming Size Plants

When plants have reached this stage in the growth cycle, several changes in the potting and post potting processes are required.

Plants that are being moved from the 2 ½" and 3" pot sizes are graded by size so they can be placed in 4" to 6" clay pots. Roots as well as back bulbs are trimmed when necessary and plants are sprayed with the same medium soaking solution.

New pots are soaked in a Physan solution. Used pots are sterilized in a 10 percent commercial bleach solution overnight and then leached in fresh water for eight hours. All stakes, drainage rocks and pot clips are soaked in a Physan solution. Potting medium is soaked in the same solution as recommended for community pots. The potting medium consists of 10 parts fir bark, 10 parts fine charcoal, 3 parts redwood chips, 5 parts medium Aliflor and 3 parts extra coarse sponge rock.

When potting the plants use clay bulb pans and fill them 1/4 full of medium pumice rock for drainage. A small amount of medium is placed in the pot over the drainage rock. The plant is positioned in the pot with the back of the rhizome placed against the pot rim and the remainder of the medium is filled in around the plant roots. Pressure is applied to the medium surface to pack the medium around the plant roots. A rhizome clip is applied to the medium surface in order to anchor the plant in the pot. In some cases the clip will need to be placed over the rhizome of the plant. In these instances we use a small piece of coconut or osmunda fiber under the clip to cushion the rhizome surface. A pot stake is then clipped to the pot lip and the plant is tied to the stake with twine to provide stabilization and a good growth pattern.

Cattleya Seedlings

Community Pots

# MUTATIONS

*Dtps. Melanie Beard-Peloric*

*C. lueddemanniana semi-alba*

*Blc. Mem. Primitiuo Miranda*

*C. lueddemanniana alba*

*C. intermedia var. aquinii*

Mutations are common in orchid populations in both species and hybrids. Mutations are the primary basis for evolution. They add variability to populations making organisms better prepared to adapt to environmental changes. Many interesting mutations occur which are used for breeding. Without the use of these mutations in breeding there would not be the diversity found in orchid hybrids.

These mutations include the peloric condition where the petals resemble lips. These are called aquinii and account for the splash petals. Alba is a condition lacking dark pigment and results in white flowers. Semi-albas lack pigment in sepals and petals. Aurea lack pigments except for yellow. In many red forms of flowers like *Rhyncostylis gigantea* and some phalaenopsis the red is actually red spots which completely cover the flowers.

Some mutations like autogamy, where the flowers self-pollinate immediately after opening, or cleistogamy, where the flower self-pollinates before opening are undesirable.

# GROWING CATTLEYAS

### Introduction

Universally popular, there is no flower that conjures an image of the essential orchid like a cattleya. Although its sovereignty is currently being challenged by the mass production of dendrobiums and phalaenopsis, the "King" Cattleya still rules the orchid family.

**Cattleya skinneri**

For convenience, we refer to the cattleyas and their next of kin as the Cattleya Alliance. Comprised of tropical and subtropical New World (western hemisphere) species, the alliance includes *Brassavola, Broughtonia, Cattleya, Encyclia, Epidendrum, Laelia, Schomburgkia, Sophronitis*, and other genera. The exciting array of colors, sizes and shapes accounts for the appeal of cattleyas. Certainly no other group of popular orchids can equal this alliance for its diversity of fragrance. From light to overwhelming, pleasant to curious, a fragrant cattleya can seduce even the most inveterate paphiopedilum grower. Not all of the

alliance depend on fragrance as an attractant for pollinators, but none can deny its power in persuading the resistant orchid buyer.

South Floridians are fortunate to enjoy a climate similar to that of the cattleya's original habitat, which is needed for success in growing most cattleyas. It is easy to duplicate their natural condition; indeed, some cattleyas can fend for themselves for years. However, the well-grown and profusely flowered specimens admired at orchid shows do not just happen. A few precepts of cattleya culture, along with observation, are essential to enjoying both the challenge of cattleya growing and the satisfaction achieved when they flower.

Sooner or later, you will hear someone's advice to grow a particular orchid "like a cattleya but with a little more..." – strong evidence of the influence cattleyas have as a point of reference. But what exactly does "grow it like a cattleya" mean?

Cattleyas are mostly epiphytic (tree dwelling) plants that require a surface to grow on or along. The surface may be a tree branch or trunk, or in some cases a rock. The important observation is that in the natural condition an epiphytic orchid's roots are exposed to the air and function as an anchoring and absorbing organ. Roots emanate from a structure called the rhizome, a kind of horizontal stem which is also the location of future growth nodes called "eyes". Rhizomes grow parallel to the surface the roots are growing on. The eye is on the side of the rhizome and will expand, forming a new shoot, which grows more or less perpendicular or upright to the rhizome.

As the shoot lengthens, three new structures are formed: a pseudobulb, a leaf and a flower sheath. The pseudobulb is a swollen stem that acts as a storage organ for water and extra carbohydrates in lean times. The leaf grows atop the pseudobulb and is the plant's main photosynthetic organ, being long, broad and flat to absorb maximum light energy from the sun. A flower sheath forms at the junction of pseudobulb and leaf. Its function is to protect the very young flower bud.

This is the general anatomical pattern that the cattleya alliance follows, with variation expressed in each member genus. Each of these cattleya structures logically reveals how they help the plant adapt to its environmental conditions.

## Light and Temperature

The conditions of light and temperature are best considered together, since their effects on plant growth are closely related. Generally speaking, an increase in light intensity or temperature will result in an increased rate of growth in a cattleya up to the point where a further increase of either would cause tissue damage.

The adaptability of cattleya orchids to a wide range of light intensities is amazing. While they can be grown and flowered acceptably under artificial light in a New Jersey basement, imagine the enhanced growth resulting from the abundance of solar light in South Florida!

Among the various species and genera, there is a level of light that is best for each. Almost all of the cattleya alliance can be grown well in 30% to 50% of full sunlight. At 50% sunlight (50% shade), during our summer months it can be bright enough for the grower to don sunglasses in the shadehouse, and yet if watering and fertilization are increased proportionately then rapid, strong plant growth results. Conversely, low light conditions yield a slow growing, weak or floppy plant with dark green leaves. Reduced light also results in reduced flowering or no flowering at all.

Adequate light can be achieved in many ways. Keep in mind that the intensity level can always be decreased by shading techniques, but if it is not adequate to begin with the outlook for strong, flowering cattleyas is dim.

Shaded areas exist all around homes and apartments, from shade trees to screened patios, from balconies to shadehouses. The possibilities are limited only by one's ingenuity. Best exposures are facing south, east or west; light problems will occur with northerly orientation. For commercial growers and hobbyists with large collections, shadehouses prove necessary. The styles of construction are limitless. Visits to some of the local growers will expose you to the various possibilities that can be incorporated into customizing a structure that fits your needs and lifestyle.

When light levels are too bright, then leaf temperature will be hot, and bleaching or burning of leaves will follow. If a leaf feels hot to the touch you

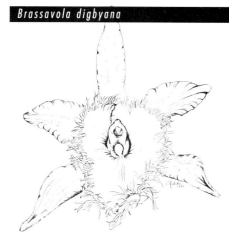

**Brassavola digbyana**

C. lueddemanniana

Laelia harpophylla

Laelia purpurata var. striata

Laelia tenebarosa

must immediately provide more shade and air circulation, and cool the leaves by misting with water. Actually, ambient temperature of 95° F is not unusual in commercial shade-houses, but this is an upper limit that requires monitoring. A cattleya hybrid with warm growing ancestry will be growing its fastest at 85-90° F, though leaf color may tend to be yellowish.

Minimum temperature limits will vary somewhat in the cattleya alliance. There are a few *Sophronitis* species that can be exposed to near freezing temperatures with no damage, but the majority of hybrids and species have little tolerance for frost conditions. Most cattleyas will endure short periods of chill at 35-40° F, but protection from cold wind is a must. A forecast of temperatures below 45° F should alert the small grower to move the collection to a warmer place. If the collection is too large for easy relocation then a tight enclosure with polyethylene film is called for, plus provision for heating the enclosure. Although South Florida experiences few cold spells during our short winter, the need for advance preparation is essential.

Cattleya plants will endure cold temperatures better if they are kept on the dry side during cold periods.

## Watering and Humidity

If is often difficult to think of orchid growing in South Florida as having water

C. amethystoglossa

problems, but the most important cultural rule in growing cattleyas is water related.

In nature, cattleya roots are exposed on the bark of a tree, seeking water in the crevasses. Breezes in the tree canopy dry the surface of the roots very quickly, but the plant is capable of storing absorbed water in several ways. The root is enclosed in a spongy layer called the velamen, storing water for later use. The pseudobulb is also a water storage organ, as are the leaves. Essentially, cattleyas have developed a marvelous system to combat periods of drought. With all this reserve capacity, it is still necessary for the roots to dry completely for them to be able to "breath" (exchange gases). Therefore, the natural pattern for roots is to dry between waterings. If the novice cattleya grower understands this concept, then all else is simple.

There will be long periods during our rainy months when cattleyas grown in containers outdoors will not be able to dry thoroughly. At these times they must be provided with shelter from the excess rain. This may be done by moving them under an overhang or building a covering over them.

A relationship that should be considered by every grower when repotting is that the potting media and container type affect the rate at which roots can dry. Some containers and mixes are chosen because they retain

Blc. Orglade's Nigrescent 'Orchidglade'

Blc. Orglade's Torchlight 'Orchid City'

Blc. RIO'S Renaissance

Blc. Janelle Tokunaga

C. aurantiaca

moisture longer; this is the case in commercial nurseries under plastic covering, for labor saving purposes. Containers and media which allow for rapid root drying are appropriate for plants growing without overhead protection from rain, or for protection from those growers who may have a heavy hand with the hose. In any situation, care must be taken to assure the roots have dried on the outside before watering. Because weather is so variable, to generalize about watering frequency (i.e., number of times per week) is to court disastrous root rot.

Achieving an optimum balance between light level, air circulation, container type and media is a challenge, but is the key to success with cattleyas or any other orchids.

Lack of humidity is not usually troublesome in South Florida! There are times in the hot months when a light sprinkling on the leaves and area around the plants with water will help cool the plant through evaporation. Naturally, low relative humidity at other times of the year can be dealt with in the same way with the exception of the few really cold, dry spells when plants should be kept dry. With experience, the devoted grower will develop a "feeling" for what is a proper humidity level.

## Containers and Media

Cattleyas and their relatives are hardy plants that can adapt to most any type of pot, basket, or slab. Various types can be established on mango trees and other trees with rough bark. These include oak, any citrus, mahogany, or tabebuia. Initially, fastening firmly so rocking does not break root tips is important. You may find heavy fishing line or old pantyhose suitable for this purpose. Clay pots are ideal for South Florida growing. You may find "orchid pots" with additional holes or slots cut along the bottom. Regular clay pots have been used, but caution must be taken to provide an air space of 1" to 2" inside the bottom by using "crock". This may be a material such as broken pieces of clay pot, or some white styrofoam packaging "peanuts". This crock layer serves the purpose of drying the media from the bottom, resulting in more abundant root growth and longer lasting medium.

Wooden "log-cabin" type baskets are used extensively in South Florida. Quite large specimens can be grown in these. Baskets commonly found are made of teak, redwood or cedar. Teak lasts longest before decomposing.

Many nurseries offer plants established onto cork slabs, tree fern or driftwood pieces, but keep in mind you will need to water and feed these plants more frequently.

Plastic pots are suitable only where complete control of watering is available. Many northern growers prefer this method; it's much cheaper on a large scale. Plastic pots can work in South Florida, but more skill is required.

That cattleyas can adapt to just about any media, organic or non-organic, is proof of their ruggedness. Remember the axiom that no matter which media or surface is employed, the roots must be allowed to dry between waterings.

Materials that have been used in South Florida include tree fern fiber, fir bark chunks, redwood chips, hardwood charcoal, various peat and sphagnum mosses, volcanic rock, Aliflor, ground cork, coconut fiber, and many others. But we can mention the most commonly used materials.

Historically, osmunda fiber, which is the root portion of a fern native to Florida, was used with much success. With time, osmunda became scarce and expensive. Tree fern fiber was a suitable substitute for osmunda and was used for decades until it too became scarce. These two materials were perfectly suited to our subtropical climate and few problems with watering frequency occurred. Today, alternatives to tree fern are being explored, which will be plentiful and economical for large scale use.

Fir bark, a by-product of the timber industry on the American west coast, has been the mainstay of orchid growers in more temperate areas for many years. Its advantages include availability and low price. It can be used in our area with a few amendments. Since it is slower to dry than tree fern or osmunda, we must incorporate materials to enhance the drying process. By adding proportions of volcanic rock, Aliflor, charcoal, or especially coarse perlite, we can make a mixture suitable for South Florida in all but the wettest periods. Commercial growers use some form of fir bark mix to grow a wide variety of orchids. Each firm will extol the virtues of its choice of media, so you can easily prompt an opinion. Listen and judge which will work in your conditions. Orchid society members are wonderful sources of information on media choice too.

Various rock derivatives have been a reliable alternative to organic media. The chief advantage of these materials is that they do not decompose over time. Generally, the frequency of watering and fertilizing must be increased. These materials make excellent media for outdoor culture.

Selection of media is a personal matter, with many variables. Careful consideration of each for your particular conditions is a long process. Experimentation and observation with different media should be done on a few plants before deciding which is best for your growing practices.

## Repotting

Without a doubt the most feared word in a novice cattleya grower's vocabulary is "repotting". It really should not be that way, but since a little effort and expense is involved, repotting is viewed as an onerous chore.

The chief reasons for repotting are that a plant has outgrown its container or the media has begun to decompose. Cattleyas can be allowed to overgrow their container by one or two growths without affecting their performance. In fact, some of the most outstanding flowerings of a cattleya may be on a growth which is actually outside the pot; the plant has been left undisturbed for a long time and is at its most established stage. But careful observation is needed to assess the physical condition of the medium.

If decomposition occurs, the medium will remain water-soaked for an unusual length of time and this can result in loss of live roots through suffocation and rot. This necessitates prompt action by repotting into fresh medium.

Experience is the teacher of the best time of year to repot, but a few generalizations can be made. Early spring is an excellent time to repot, since days grow longer and warmer. Some growers observe the initiation of new roots as a signal to repot, but this can be at various stages of growth or time of year, depending on variety and parentage.

The actual technique of repotting

Slc. Orient Amber

Sc. Beaufort

Blc. Diane Katherine Sauleda

is unique to the individual grower, each being used successfully. The purpose, though, remains constant, to give the roots fresh material to grow in.

The skills of repotting can be learned by taking a class or by being taught by a grower at their nursery. Hands-on experience is priceless; for all the variables involved with repotting each plant cannot be visualized in text. Doing is the best teacher!

## Fertilizing

No topic in all of horticulture is as controversial as plant nutrition. Every grower has a different opinion on the correct ratio, amount, timing, etc. of their fertilizing regime. And if one listens to all the arguments an overwhelming bewilderment is likely to result.

In practice, feeding cattleyas can be as complicated as you can endure or as simple as you please.

Cattleya species growing in rain forests are not heavy feeders. Their nutrition comes in liquid form, dissolved in rain water. While rain does contain some nutrients and minerals, it acts chiefly to bathe roots in a solution which contains chemical elements from animal droppings and decomposing leaves, in very dilute doses. There is nothing complicated about that scenario. The key insight is that cattleyas like to be fed as often as they are watered, with all the elements they need at a low concentration.

Laelia pupurata var. carnea

Being cattleyas, though, they can endure the extremes of our eccentric fertilizing regimes. Therefore, if you do not have the patience to feed at every watering then at least give a dose of fertilizer every third or fourth watering. At a reduced frequency the rate applied is full strength of soluble fertilizer per gallon of water. If you are feeding at least once a week you can use $\frac{1}{4}$ to $\frac{1}{2}$ of that strength. An occasional flushing of the media with clear water will avoid the gradual buildup of mineral salts, a potential danger.

Most organic and inorganic potting media will dictate the use of one of the balanced ratio formulations, i.e. 1-1-1. This means a 20-20-20 or 15-15-15 analysis can be applied and the plant will be well fed. If the chosen media contains primarily fir bark, a higher percentage of nitrogen is needed, hence 30-10-10 analysis is recommended for the main course.

The blossom booster formulations are for occasional use in the late summer or early fall. Use of these is not at all mandatory if the plant is healthy and has the opportunity to build a reserve of carbohydrates for flowering. Remember a weakened plant will not flower no matter which fertilizer analysis it is given.

The use of coated time-release fertilizer pellets is not a good idea for the novice to try. Nutrient levels are too low, and the excessive application of these pellets has

*Schomburgkia humboltii*

*C. skinneri*

*C. skinneri alba*

*Laelia briegeri*

led to the demise of many an orchid through the burning of roots.

Another common short cut should be avoided: the practice of submerging a collection of plants in a bucket of dilute fertilizer solution. The not-so-apparent risk in this practice is the ease with which diseases can be spread by the solution from an infected plant to subsequent plants being fed this way. Better to pour a small amount through the container and not reuse the runoff.

**C. Iris**

## Pests

When Ponce de Leon named Florida "the land of flowers", he probably forgot that with flowers come insects – so an appropriate but not as appealing alternate name could have been "the land of insects". A familiarity with the assortment of native pests is a rite of passage for the bona fide well-rounded South Floridian.

Chief among the cattleya pests are the numerous varieties of scale insects. These insidious critters can literally suck the life from plant cells, leaving tell-tale yellow patches which eventually turn brown (i.e., dead). Vigilance is required and an arsenal of chemical weapons is available. Probably the easiest method of reducing nearly all scale infestations is by physically scrubbing them away with an old soft toothbrush. One must be diligent and remove the dried sheathing that covers the pseudobulb. This papery membrane is called cataphyll. After this scrubbing step, the wise use of appropriate chemical solutions according to label instructions may be called for. There are non-toxic alternatives to chemicals which produce equally effective results, and their use is encouraged.

Other minor pests of cattleyas include mites, mealy bugs, aphids, ants, roaches, snails and slugs. An observant grower can easily discover signs of these unwelcome visitors while watering or fertilizing.

A grower's library is not complete without the invaluable Orchid Pests and Diseases handbook published by the American Orchid Society. This is required reading. Your plants will be testing your knowledge.

## Diseases

Cattleyas can become ill from many diseases. It is, however, much easier to maintain the health of plants if we understand conditions that give diseases a chance to start.

Almost all plant fungal and bacterial diseases can be traced back to careless watering practices. An experienced knack of knowing when a cattleya is dry enough to water is the essence of disease control. It's as simple as that.

Once a disease has begun, a myriad of possible remedies can be tried. First, though, the disease must be correctly identified, and again you are referred to the treatment given in the Orchid Pests and Diseases handbook.

Viral diseases are another problem that we can encounter. Much experience and knowledge is necessary in identifying viruses, since symptoms are not always apparent and infection does not usually result in the plant's demise. Strict adherence to sanitation of cutting tools and other objects that physically contact plants is essential.

Knowledgeable orchid hobbyists can minimize the incidence of pests or diseases by purchasing their orchids from a nursery known for the health of its plants and the guarantee that accompanies the purchase. A neat and sanitary nursery is obvious at first glance and the plants offered usually reflect a caring, knowledgeable grower.

## Conclusion

Now that we have a brief description of the important elements in successfully growing and flowering cattleyas, it is up to you to apply them to your plants. A lot of accumulated knowledge and experience is reflected each time a healthy cattleya blooms. The material presented here is only a brief glimpse of how to "grow it like a cattleya". Those of us who have grown and loved cattleyas for many years know that the newness of learning from our plants is never finished. We wish you the same enjoyment.

*Brassavola nodosa*

# GROWING VANDACEOUS ORCHIDS

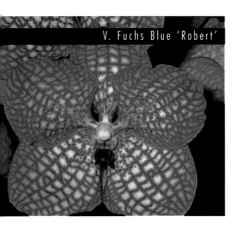
V. Fuchs Blue 'Robert'

Ascda. Fuchs Honeycomb

V. Joan Vigiani

The objectives of good orchid culture are to promote robust, disease-free plants with high quality blooms. These goals are especially important for vandaceous orchids which produce quality flowers only from strong plants.

The vandaceous orchids which we will discuss fall mainly into the genera of *Vanda*, *Ascocentrum* and Ascocenda *(Vanda X Ascocentrum)*. For the purpose of culture, we may continue to treat *Euanthe sanderiana*, the reclassified species from which most of our popular vandaceous hybrids originated, in the genus *Vanda*.

When considering the cultural requirements of vandaceous plants, it is important to remember that all vandaceous orchids are of monopodial growth habit. This type grows from the tip, or crown, of the plant. Lateral buds are present on the main stem and these may develop into plantlets when the plant has attained sufficient size and strength to support them. In accordance with the growth habit of the main stem, each plantlet will also continue to grow indefinitely from its tip. The inflorescences of vandaceous monopodial orchids emanate from the axils of the leaves which are arranged in two rows or ranks. The stem spaces between leaves are extremely variable in size, from less than an inch to several inches apart.

Vandaceous orchids can be further categorized by leaf shape into three groups with somewhat different cultural needs. These are: strap-leaved, terete, and semi-terete.

**Strap-leaved plants** have flat, leathery leaves. This category includes such vanda species as *coerulea, dearei, luzonica, merrillii, tricolor* and *sanderiana*, as well as the ascocentrums.

Chtra. Fuchs Precious

Aerctm. Fuchs Gem

Rhy. retusa

Rhy. gigantea 'Fuchs Spots'

Rhy. coelestis

**Terete** orchids have tapering, pencil-shaped leaves which are circular in transverse cross-section. The most common species in this group are *V. teres* and *V. hookeriana*.

**Semi-teretes**, as they are referred to here, are a hybrid combination with some terete species in the background. Their leaves are somewhat pencil-shaped and tapered but not always completely round in cross-section.

## Cultural Requirements

Cultural requirements can be generally summarized in the five categories of temperature, water or humidity, light, air movement, and fertilizer. We will consider each category individually as it applies to vandaceous orchids:

**Temperature** - Vandaceous orchids grow best under daytime conditions of 65° F or higher, but can withstand long spells of hot weather and short spells of cold. They will continue in active growth anytime of the year if given warm temperatures and bright light.

Night temperatures should not generally be lower than 55° F. We have seen some vandaceous plants withstand temperatures as low as 38° F for 2-3 hours with damage to root tips and flower buds, but not to the plant itself. It is most important to protect plants from air movement during brief periods of extreme cold.

**Terete Vanda**

**Light** - The strap-leaved types can be grown indoors, in greenhouse conditions. With high humidity, maximum sunlight should be given with only enough shade to keep the temperature within the appropriate range. For our greenhouses in South Florida we use 46% shade cloth covered with 6 mil plastic on the top and sides of greenhouses, producing about 50% shade.

Terete vandas and their semi-terete hybrids are sun lovers. Not only will they flower year round in tropical areas, they are also floriferous in the subtropics. They can be grown in the full sun and are ideal for landscape use.

**Air Movement** - In the greenhouse, under summer sun, vigorous air movement from a fan is important to keep leaf temperature down and avoid cell damage from heat. As mentioned previously, it is important to restrict air movement under colder temperatures.

**Water** - A high daytime humidity is essential, especially on sunny days, and misting once or twice a day in bright weather will be helpful. On hot, sunny days around 80% humidity is appropriate. Water sparingly in winter, during long cloudy spells, or after repotting. In any season, avoid watering plants late in the afternoon. Vandaceous plants should be dry before nightfall.

In addition to the natural elements of temperature, air and water, good culture of vandaceous orchids also requires some help from man-made supplies: containers, potting media, insecticides, fungicides, and fertilizers.

**Fertilizing** - Vandaceous orchids are heavy feeders. Once a week during the growing season, plants should be given a solution of a complete fertilizer. High-nitrogen fertilizers should not be used on vandaceous plants as they will inhibit flowering. All plants should be flushed thoroughly with plain water once a week to remove built-up salts. If using an automatic proportioner, plants may be fertilized as often as daily with a more dilute solution. Whatever feeding plan you follow, remember, it is important to be faithful to the regimen you have established.

Use 20-20-20 fertilizer weekly during the growing season. Inside the greenhouse, under a controlled environment, the concentration is the standard recommended one. During the winter non-growing season, apply the same proportions every two weeks rather than weekly. In addition, at every third feeding substitute 10-30-20. This substitution applies to plants in all seasons of the year. Further, once a month add ¼ teaspoon of SUPERthrive, a concentrated vitamin and hormone solution for plants, to each gallon of fertilizer solution.

**Potting** - Vandaceous plants will grow well in any porous medium if properly aerated. Tree-fern chunks, coarse bark or charcoal are good choices. The roots should not be smothered by tight potting or soggy medium. Wooden baskets are preferred, but pots can be used if drainage is good. If potting in baskets, those made of teak are the best choice as they will last the longest. If teak is not available redwood is a good second choice, and cedar a third option. Use 4" teak baskets for the first two years after seedling size, 6" baskets for the next two years, and 8" baskets for mature plants. Plants should be suspended so that the aerial roots are free; otherwise, the roots attach themselves to the bench or wall and are damaged when the plants are moved. Recently potted plants should be maintained under slightly more shaded conditions until they are established.

Because vandaceous plants have large aerial roots, they do not like to be disturbed by removal from their container. Therefore, we "elevate" plants from smaller to larger baskets. This step-up procedure is accomplished by soaking the roots briefly in water

**Vanda teres**

Ascda. Fuchs Mandarin

Ascda. Fuchs Angel Frost 'Michael'

Opst. Ruben 'R. F. Orchid'

until they become pliable. Roots are then worked through the slats in the larger basket as the old smaller basket and plant are placed intact in the larger basket. Never coil the roots around the old basket because vandaceous plants will feed better with an unrestricted root system. A few large pieces of charcoal can be added to hold the smaller basket securely within the larger, or wiring the smaller basket into the larger will accomplish the same result. This method minimizes shock to the plant and permits continued, uninterrupted growth. Adding SUPERthrive to the water used to soak the plant will further minimize its shock and seems to encourage faster growth of new roots.

There are occasions, however, when disturbing the roots cannot be avoided, e.g. a rotten basket, or repotting of plants grown in pots. These plants should be soaked in water, removed as carefully as possible, and placed in a solution of vitamins/hormones and fungicide, allowed to soak 5 minutes and then potted in a new basket.

The best season for the potting or repotting of vandaceous plants is late spring to early summer, but these orchids may be repotted at almost anytime of the year.

Since vandaceous orchids grow rapidly with good light, water and regular fertilizing,

Asctm. miniatum

V. tessellata aurea 'Fuchs Lemonade'

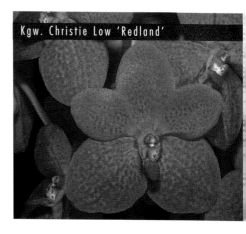

Kgw. Christie Low 'Redland'

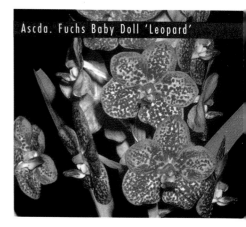

Ascda. Fuchs Baby Doll 'Leopard'

seedlings should be grown in 3" pots, using a mix of fine charcoal and tree fern fiber, and loosely potted. Seedlings should be kept in slightly more shaded conditions than mature plants, but included in the same water and fertilizer programs. Humidity and good air movement should be maintained.

**Landscaping** - Terete vandas can be used beautifully in tropical and subtropical landscapes.

To prepare a "potted" arrangement, we create a tall wire cylinder as a support; tying cuttings around the outside. The support is then placed in a large terracotta pot with 3" of coarse lava rock in the bottom. Then 4"-5" of peat moss is added. These orchids can also be used to great effect in beds or along fences using any coarse material for the bed and tying plants securely to supports. Keep in mind that teretes and many semi-teretes will only bloom from the top portion of plants that have reached the full height of their supporting structure. It is better not to use tall walls or trees as support for these types of plants.

**Propagation** - Given the right cultural treatment to encourage strong plants, many vandaceous orchids will produce lateral growths referred to as keikis. A grower may force a plant toward keiki generation by

Vanda *sanderiana*

Illustration from
Veitch's *Manual of
Orchidaceous Plants*

removing the top part of the plant, or apex, which then becomes a propagation. The top "cutting" should have at least 2 or 3 strong roots, approximately 3"-4" long, before its removal from the plant. In time, latent lateral buds at various points along the main stem of the mother plant are awakened. These side shoots will eventually produce roots and when of appropriate size, the shoots can be separated from the main plant by removal with a sharp, sterilized knife. After treating the incisions of both the mother plant and the keikis with a paste of fungicide, these propagations may then be potted in the normal manner.

**Pests & Diseases** - An important aspect of good culture, is the maintenance of an orchid collection free from disease and pests. In general, all new acquisitions should be carefully inspected before adding them to your collection. Benches and floors should be kept clean and free of debris. Plants should be watered only when necessary, and time allowed for them to dry between watering. Regular fertilizing strengthens the plants. Each plant in the collection should be inspected regularly for any signs of disease or pests, and necessary action taken before the problem becomes acute.

One of the most common, and annoying pests which infest vandaceous plants is thrips. These are very small sucking insects about 1 mm in size. Damage usually occurs on flowers and buds, causing the blooms to rapidly lose their beauty. These airborne insects seem to prosper in flowering trees and shrubs. In tropical areas thrips are a problem year around. When thrips become a problem, a spraying program must be followed as plants come into bud. Once the thrips get inside the flower bud, they are protected from contact sprays. A fine spray mist should be used to avoid injuring tender buds. As a preventive, spray spikes and buds with a solution of Sevin, following manufacturer's directions. If flowers are open, spray directly with Orthene soluble powder, which does not damage the blooms.

Scale is another pest which may attack vandaceous plants. It is usually detected on the leaves and may be indicated by yellowing of the infected area. Scales are insects, generally round and flattened or globular in shape. Scales not only injure the plants by their feeding, but they also secrete a honeylike substance on which sooty mold may grow. Scale eggs are maintained beneath the female insect. Each female may produce several hundred eggs which hatch at different intervals. Therefore, additional applications of insecticide must be given to control the newly hatched scale. Use Orthene soluble powder or Malathion.

Ants are common insects which are not directly harmful to orchid plants. However, ants may be a carrying agent of scale and therefore should be controlled. Ants can be deterred by preventive use of general orchid insecticides.

Slugs and snails are not generally a problem with vandaceous orchids grown in baskets. However, if present, they may damage new roots. If a problem develops, they can be effectively eliminated using Metaldehyde Baits as directed by the manufacturer.

Bacterial brown spot is a disease which is sometimes found in the crown of vandaceous plants. It is identified by small, pinpoint-sized spots sprinkled over the new leaf. To control this disease, use Physan 20.

Sclerotium rot (sometimes referred to as crown rot) also attacks vandaceous plants. This fungus normally begins at the crown of the plant, but may spread to the main stem and/or roots. The affected parts become yellow and then become soft, turning brown and then drying out. If not stopped, the rot will eventually kill the entire plant. This fungus should be treated by pulling the affected center leaves out of the crown. Then the crown should be sprayed with Physan 20 (fungicide) solution. Finally, a paste of fungicide powder, vitamin/hormone, and water should be applied to the affected area(s). Use Dithane and SUPERthrive. The damaged crown should begin to regenerate and the plant begin to grow again from the center. Even if the crown does not regenerate, there is a strong likelihood that the plant will produce keikis.

A relatively new fungal disease now seen frequently is Phyllosticta Leaf Spot. This fungus, first recognized in Thailand, is much more serious than initially believed. Affected plants will die prematurely if early warning signs are ignored. The fungus produces rough-feeling lesions which appear as eye-shaped spots on the leaves. These will usually, over time, merge to a single large infected patch. The affected leaves will eventually turn brown and drop off. By the time the disease reaches this stage, its spores have already spread to surrounding areas and plants. Because there is no fungicide yet proven to cure this disease, control of the fungus is critical. All affected leaves should be removed and burned. The plant should then be sprayed with Dithane. Although this will not eliminate the fungus, it seems to slow its progress. The best precaution is to carefully examine all vandaceous plants before introducing

Neost. Lou Sneary 'Sweetheart'

them into your collection. This disease is highly contagious and spreads quickly to other plants.

When using any fungicides or insecticides, it is important to follow the manufacturers recommendations for the correct proportions. Remember, the manufacturer recommends the maximum amounts. You may often solve your problem using lesser solutions. Overuse of chemicals, including pesticides and fungicides, can be very dangerous to your plants, the environment and yourself. The best prevention of pests and diseases is the maintenance of a clean, well cared for environment with strong, healthy plants.

The vandaceous orchids are among the easiest to grow and they produce the widest range of color, and the most floriferous plants, of any of the orchid genera.

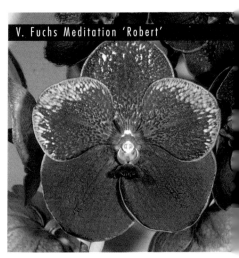
V. Fuchs Meditation 'Robert'

Aranda Noorah Alsagoff (purple)

# GROWING DENDROBIUMS

Growing dendrobiums in South Florida can be fun and a rewarding addition to your orchid collection. For the most part, they are easy to grow, flower often, and make beautiful specimen plants.

The genus *Dendrobium* is among the largest genus in the orchid family. The exact amount of species cannot be agreed upon, but there are as many as 1,400, spread around the Old World. This makes for an exciting array of possibilities.

The range is vast, extending from India eastwards to Japan and south to Australia and Fiji. They are basically epiphytes or tree dwellers. In fact, the name dendrobium is made up of two Greek words, *dendron* -tree and *bios* -life, referring to this epiphytic habit. The only other similarity that unites all the species in the genus is the structure of the pollen.

After noting these similarities, the diversity of the genus must be mentioned. It is truly mind-boggling. The dendrobiums can range from warm growing lowlands to cool growing high elevations. The growths can be tight clusters of miniatures or monstrous canes exceeding 9'. The flowers range in all colors and shapes, flowering on long inflorescences or clustered along the cane.

Many of these diverse plants of dendrobium can be grown here. Now that you know the variety available to be grown you must be asking "How can I begin to understand such a large group?"

The easiest way to begin is to understand the difference between species and hybrids. Species are those found in the jungle or in their native habitat. Hybrids are the

Den. bigibbum

Den. fimbriatum var. occulatum

Den. stratiotes

Finally, growing dendrobiums will take you to into the exotic realms of the species. Here is where more specialized knowledge of each species will make the job easier and more rewarding. The easiest way to tackle this knowledge is to begin with a general understanding of the 'sections' of dendrobiums. This is a convenient way to divide the genus into groups that can be recognized by some distinctive character or peculiarity that is easily noticed.

Although this subject is enough to fill volumes of books, a brief overview of the sections most commonly seen in South Florida is necessary. A few examples of each are given.

**PHALAENANTHE** - (*phalaenopsis, bigibbum, affine, williamsianum*) - This section contains the species most often sought after for full, round shaped flowers borne on long inflorescences. The plants have upright canes and the old ones tend to become leafless, but often continue to flower, therefore do not cut them off! Most of this type flowers in the autumn and require tropical conditions (60° F minimum nights) that have a definite dry rest period after flowering.

**SPATULATA** - Formerly known as Ceratobium (*gouldii, lineale, antennatum, taurinum, canaliculatum, lasianthera,*) - Commonly known as 'antelope' type, because their flower petals are twisted and curling like the antlers of an antelope. Most have long lasting flowers and the canes are capable of bearing many inflorescences throughout their lives. Many of the species grow at sea level in hot and humid situations, often overhanging rivers or near the seashore. This makes them perfect candidates for South Florida. Since they are warm growing tropical plants, give them plenty of water and fertilizer in the summer and if the winter night temperatures remain 55° F or above

results of cross-pollination of these species to produce varying results such as increased vigor, size, number of flowers or better colors. Sometimes a hybrid appears that is superior to others and then a process called cloning is done. These 'clones' are then available in large quantities for everyone.

Generally, the dendrobiums that you find in the garden centers of large retailers are clones. They are an excellent way to begin growing dendrobiums. You will soon see how common this type of plant is and then you will want to try some more unusual hybrids available from excellent orchid specialty nurseries in South Florida. You will then be assured that your plants will thrive in the same climate.

they only need a minimal rest period. The colder it gets, the drier the plants should be.

**CALLISTA** - (*aggregatum, chrysotoxum, farmeri, densiflorum*) This section is represented by very distinct looking plants that have bulbs growing closely together with thick leathery leaves. The flowers are attractive, pendent (hanging down) 'bunches'. Very popular for the showy brightly colored flowers, they are grown and available widely even though the flowers are short-lived. Give these plants a strong rest in winter by giving them cooler temperatures and just enough water to keep the bulbs from shriveling, no fertilizer is necessary. Even in the summer the plants require only medium amounts of water and fertilizer. They grow best mounted on tree fern slabs or in baskets.

**DENDROBIUM** - (*superbum, fimbriatum, parishii, nobile, wardianum*) The plants in this section are sometimes referred to as the 'soft cane' type of dendrobiums. The stems are fleshy and cane-like or slender and pendulous. The inflorescences are in little bundles of 1-5 flowers that bloom along leafless canes. Most of these plants require bright light in winter with chilly temperatures. They will drop many of their leaves before flowering, so do not panic! Nobile types require almost no water or fertilizer at this time of year.

**LATOUREA** - (*atroviolaceum, macrophyllum, spectabile, forbesii*) - These plants are robust growers from New Guinea. The leaves are large and leathery and generally remain evergreen. The group has unusual flowers that range from bizarre to beautiful. Some are covered with hairs. Flowers tend to be very long lasting. Check the culture of the species individually as some come from high elevations. The culture would be similar to the antelope types.

**FORMOSAE** - formally Nigrohirsutae (*formosum, dearil, sanderae, draconis*) - This group is distinguished by the short black hairs on the canes. The flowers are mostly white and are generally large with 2-3 borne together in clusters along the cane. Many of these take cool winter night temperatures. Keep on dry side in winter and grow vigorously in summer.

As previously mentioned 'generalizations' are difficult, but overall here are the basics for growing dendrobiums in South Florida.

**LIGHT** - Strong indirect light or shade cloth between 45% to 55% shade is recommended. Some plants can be acclimatized to more light in a

Den. Autumn Carnival 'Karen'

Den. chrysotoxum

Den. moschatum

landscape situation, but light levels should be increased gradually and good air movement is necessary to keep the leaves from burning.

**WATER** - Depending how much drainage is in the medium, dendrobiums can take large amounts of water during summer when they are in active growth and should never shrivel. If rain persists for several days while the new growths are young and tender, an application of fungicide may be necessary. Plant growth is always less with shorter days and cooler temperatures, so less water and fertilizer is needed. Remember to check individual species for severe rest period requirements.

**FERTILIZER** - In active growth, plants need balanced 20-20-20 applications on a regular basis since most potting media have little nutrients. Switch to a blossom booster when growths are mature to encourage flowering. As with water the hotter and brighter it is, the more fertilizer needed. Reduce in winter, to as little as none depending on type.

**TEMPERATURE** - South Florida temperatures are suited for growing the warm to intermediate dendrobiums. Caution is needed for the occasional cold front that comes from an arctic blast. Tropical plants will suffer and should be brought inside or protected by artificial heat.

**POTTING** - There are many types of potting media available for use on dendrobiums. Gravel or lava rock can be used and is good for reducing root rot disease and repotting. However, you must increase water and fertilizer since no nutrients are available in this inert medium. Bark and charcoal mixes are good, but in the heat and humidity of South Florida, potting every year is almost essential as this mix breaks down quickly. Investigate your own options for your environment, but be sure to adjust water accordingly. An important reminder is never to 'overpot' dendrobiums. They seem to thrive and flower better in small pots.

**BUD BLAST** - This is one problem that seems to affect dendrobiums more than other genera of orchids. Several things can cause this phenomenon, which is when the buds turn yellow and fall off before opening into flowers. One is genetic that we cannot control. This essentially means that the cross has a flaw. The other cause is culture. Some dendrobiums are more sensitive to changes in their environment than others. In other words 'stress' can be caused from such things as temperature changes or water patterns. It is generally better to avoid water on the buds when the plants are in spike.

Because we are lucky enough to live in South Florida, it makes growing easy since our seasons are similar to the basic requirements found in other tropical regions of the world. Dendrobiums from high mountain elevations should be avoided or approached with caution.

Dendrobiums can be as easy or as challenging as you want them to be. Plants can be placed in the landscape by hanging on a patio, placing around the pool, or even attaching them to trees. Optimum culture and nurturing can be done and the rewards can be a payoff of extra flowers on a specimen sized plant or even an award or blue ribbon from the orchid society.

Den. Jiad Gold

Den. thyrsiflorum

Den. parishii

# GROWING PHALAENOPSIS

## INTRODUCTION

Phalaenopsis also called "moth orchid" derives its name from the Greek word *phaluna* meaning moth and *opsis* meaning resembling due to the flowers similarity to some tropical moths. Known as mariposa or butterflies in the Philippines and as Moon Orchids in Indonesia, phalaenopsis are an excellent orchid for the beginner since they are somewhat simple to grow. In our beautiful climate of South Florida the peak flowering season for phalaenopsis is from December to March.

One subdivision of *Phalaenopsis* called Euphalaenopsis, offers large, spray-type flowers. With beautiful flowers that can last for 2 to 5 months, their nearly continuous blooms can be achieved by good culture and careful pruning of the flower spike. It is not uncommon to see large branching sprays with 15 to 25 flowers. After the stem has finished flowering, it can be pruned back to the first faded flower and the node just below the pruned stem will develop a side spray if the plant and flower spike are strong. Flowers on a side spray can open in approximately 3 to 4 months and present blooms during the summer (though they are generally smaller blooms than the blooms on the original spray.) This is not always recommend since the following year's flowers are often smaller because the plant has expended quite a bit of energy to produce the second branch and has not had a chance to rest.

The second subdivision of *Phalaenopsis* called Stauroglottis, offer smaller colorful flowers that are usually spotted or barred. With their petals all the same size or smaller

than their sepals, the lip is devoid of appendages (though in some species the lip is decorated with hair or calli.) Stauroglottis generally flower from April to September.

With approximately fifty species of phalaenopsis, not all are well known in cultivation. More and more, orchidists are hybridizing the rarer phalaenopsis for their uniquely colorful flowers.

The foliage of phalaenopsis is attractive with long, succulent, broad, curving leaves. Quite shiny, the leaves range from plain to mottled green with grayish-green or purple on the underside of the leaves. The leaves of a mature phalaenopsis can range from 4" to 15". Generally they only grow 1 to 2 leaves a year and mature plants usually have 5 or 6 leaves though some plants may produce more.

Roots often look flattened and can appear from the stem between leaves, growing down into the pot or traveling great lengths.

## CULTURAL REQUIREMENTS

**LIGHT** - Best grown in low light for 6 to 12 hours a day until ready to spike, you can initiate blooming by increasing the length of light exposure to 24 hours. Leaves should feel cool to the touch especially during periods of high light. Since phalaenopsis do not actively grow in winter they can tolerate high light at this time and it does not seem to stress the plants. In summer new leaves should be kept from excess light as severe sunburn can kill the plant. It is recommended to use shade cloth of 85-90% shade during the summer.

**TEMPERATURE** - Though the ideal temperature for phalaenopsis is 70-85°F. Plants can tolerate temperatures much higher for short periods of time. Luckily here in

Phal. Mem. Elizabeth Meade 'Ruben'

Dtps. Red Beard

Phal. (Joey x Wilma Hughes)

South Florida we often experience brief cold snaps during the winter months. Cold snaps induce the spiking and eventual flowering of phalaenopsis. They can withstand temperatures of 50° F without damaging the plants. It is important to winterize your shade house with plastic especially on the north and west sides. If temperatures are predicted to be lower than 50° F, heaters or all night sprinkling will keep phalaenopsis safe. Be sure to continue either procedure until the air temperature the following day goes up to 60° F.

**WATER** - Phalaenopsis should be watered frequently and the medium never allowed to become completely dry. Frequent watering is necessary but plants should be kept from staying too wet. An indicator of proper watering is to look at the plant's root tips.

Green root tips indicate adequate moisture levels, while white root tips mean a need for more water. Phalaenopsis roots are the plant's only means of water storage and should never become dehydrated. Never allow water to stand on the leaves especially at night. This encourages many problems

Dtps. George Moler 'Ruben'

including *Phytophthora caxtorum* (fungus), black rot, crown rot and damping off. Watering in the morning allows the moisture to evaporate completely before nightfall. Plants love a light mist of water during the day.

**AIR MOVEMENT AND VENTILATION** - Air movement and ventilation are critical, especially here in South Florida. Our high temperatures and humidity require fans to be strategically placed in your shade house for the plants to thrive. The importance of good ventilation and air circulation cannot be stressed too strongly. Air circulation helps your plants resist diseases such as the spotting of flowers by *Botrytis cinerea* (fungus) and helps leaf surfaces to dry after the morning watering. Good air circulation helps reduce the risk of sunburn by keeping the leaf temperature cool and avoiding the damage that excessive heat can create.

FEEDING - Every orchidist has their own secret fertilizing formula. Careful observation of your phalaenopsis will be a good guide. The frequency and concentration of your formula must be adjusted to suit their specific needs. A recommended balanced

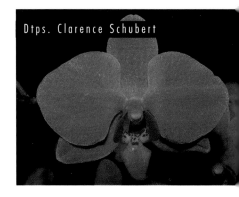

Dtps. Clarence Schubert

Phal. Hilo Lip

Phal. Florida Snow

Phal. Tiger Butter

formula of 20-20-20 applied to plants weekly seems to work quite well. In addition, it is recommended to add SUPERthrive to the 20-20-20 formula. Once a month a mixture of 30-10-10 is used since phalaenopsis seem to need extra nitrogen. In late October or early November, change your formula to 9-45-15, until the plants are in full bloom.

On seedlings, a high phosphate formula such as 9-45-15 for 3 to 6 weeks can be used or until signs of good roots show. Again add SUPERthrive to the 9-45-15 formula.

All fertilizing should be stopped until the plants have been repotted after the old flowering spikes have been cut (spring or early summer).

*IMPORTANT - Phalaenopsis (and most orchids), achieve maximum absorption of nutrients and micronutrients (trace minerals) when the pH of your fertilizer is at 5.5. To achieve this balance, you may need to add the necessary amounts of acid. (see chart on page 15.)*

**REPOTTING AND MEDIUM** - Phalaenopsis LOVE TO BE REPOTTED. The preferred medium is sphagnum moss. The following simple steps will ensure great phalaenopsis. First, make sure you do not use old pots. Used pots can be contaminated. If you must use old pots they must be sterilized in a strong bleach solution for 24 hours (one cup per gallon). Rinse the pots well and allow to dry in the sun. Take the sphagnum moss you are going to use and soak it in water. Drain excess water so that the sphagnum moss is damp.

Starting with a clean pot fill $1/3$ with styrofoam peanuts. Be careful not to confuse with the new biodegradable peanuts that are made from corn starch. You will end up with a soggy mess.

Thoroughly soak the plant that is to be

repotted and let it sit for a few minutes. This will cause the roots that may be attached to the pot to swell and loosen their grip. Gently move the stubborn attached roots with your fingers. Take the plant that is to be repotted, gently turn upside down holding the base of the plant between your fingers and the pot should slide off. Be careful not to damage the roots. Remove all the old medium and gently spray with water to clean excess debris. Take clean, sterilized clippers and cut all old dried and rotting roots away. Spray the roots, the plant and the sphagnum moss with Physan 20. Gently pack sphagnum around the center of the plant leaving roots hanging around the ball of sphagnum. Lightly pack the sphagnum over the remaining roots EXCEPT for about ½" from the bottom of root lengths. This allows for a few root tips to easily dig their way into the peanuts. Center the plant in the pot and make sure the sphagnum does not cover the base of the plant where the roots are attached just under the leaves.

Sphagnum moss should be fluffy and not hard packed in the pot. Fill in any spaces around the pot with additional sphagnum.

**DISEASE AND PEST CONTROL** - A regular regimen of Physan 20 will help control bacterial and fungal diseases. Physan 20 is recommend not only for spraying plants but benches and walkways as well.

For pest control such as mites, mealy bugs, thrips and scale use the following: Mites (often called spider mites) — Insecticidal Soap; for thrips — Orthene; and for scale and mealy bugs — Sevin. Use the rates recommended by the manufacturer for your particular problem.

Treating mites once or twice is usually not enough to control the pests. It is often necessary to make 3 to 4 applications repeated at intervals every 7 to 10 days. Hosing off plants can wash away mites and break down their webs.

Mealy bugs appear as white cotton looking masses. Repeat applications to control overlapping generations. Thrips which are barely visible, often hide deep in buds and are difficult to eradicate. Spraying should be repeated to control overlapping generations.

Slugs and snails are nocturnal but shiny slime trails confirm their presence. They may be baited with beer or a cut potato. Commercial baits are also available. Nighttime visits with a flashlight and close examination of your plants can reveal these pests.

# GROWING
# THE LADY SLIPPERS

Paph. Julius

Slipper orchids, commonly referred to as "lady slippers," are a large group of primarily terrestrial orchids with pouched shaped lips. There are four genera in this group: *Cypripedium, Phragmipedium, Paphiopedalum,* and *Selenipedilum* (a seldom seen group of plants one to seven meters tall). The cypripediums are our own "Jack in the pulpits," found in forests, bogs, and fields throughout parts of North America and Europe. The phragmipediums are native to Central and South America. Paphiopedalums are from Asia and several Pacific islands.

Although cypripediums may be familiar from our childhood, they are not readily cultivated out of their native habitat. They tend to be perennials that die back in the winter and sprout up in the spring. They have very specific soil requirements, perhaps even to the point of requiring a specific microrhyza fungus in their soils. As with all wild slipper orchids, this genus is protected by law and may not be removed from the wild. A few hybrids have been made in this group, but are not readily available. However many other types of slipper orchids are grown commercially and are available through numerous sources.

## Phragmipediums

The phragmipediums are probably one of the best orchids for the hobbyist to grow. They have minimal light requirements, like to be kept moist like many house plants, and often flower for up to 18 months on a single stem. The first hybrids of phragmipediums were made in the late 19th century. Given the limited number of species in this group, with colors mainly in white, green, brown and pink, and the fact that, unlike other orchids, slippers will not breed outside their own genus, the variety of flowers was quite limited. The dozen or so hybrids registered before 1990, fell into three groups; long petaled *P. caudatum* hybrids, somewhat shorter petaled *P. longifolium* type hybrids, and wide petaled *P. schlimii* hybrids. The discovery and introduction of the red to orange *P. besseae* in the 1980's has caused an infusion of hybrids with new colors into this group.

**Phragmipedium caudatum hybrids:** By far the most spectacular of all phragmipediums because of its extremely long petals, often reaching over two feet in length, *P. caudatum* and its hybrids are always an incredible sight in flower. Flower color ranges from green and white, to rich mahogany tones. The hybrids all share the characteristic long downward trailing petals. The inflorescence will normally last for two to three months at a time. Phragmipedium Grande is one of the best known hybrids.

**Phragmipedium longifolium type hybrids:** *Phragmipedium longifolium* produces tall, successively blooming inflorescences. Its long outstretched petals are often outlined in a rosy pink. The rest of the flower is mainly shades of green and white. The stems will usually reach two to four feet in length, flowering over a 12 to 18 month period. The long petals and stem habit are carried through in its hybrids. Several other species have the same flowering habit and produce similar characteristics in their hybrids: *P. caricinum, P. pearcii, and P. boissierianum.*

**The Brazilian Phragmipediums;** *Phragmipedium sargentianum, P. lindleyanum,* and *P. vittatum,* offer tall stems and orange to red coloration. In hybrids this coloration usually

Paph. armeniacum

Paph. Evelyn Rolke

only shows up along the edges of the petals to highlight the flowers. One of the more striking recent hybrids from this group is P. Sorcerer's Apprentice (P. sargentianum x P. longifolium) with long outward stretched, twisted orange-red petals.

**Phragmipedium schlimii hybrids**: *Phragmipedium schlimii* is a small-flowered successive bloomer from Colombia of compact growth. The flowers are rosy pink with a white center and a yellow staminode. It has a very dominant effect in the overall color of its hybrids. They all are pink to rose, often with a white center to the flowers. Their successively blooming characteristics are dominant, but somewhat reduced when crossed with P. caudatum types. Phragmipedium Sedenii, a cross with P. longifolium, is probably the best known and most commonly grown of phragmipedium hybrids. Divisions of the many early clones have been propagated for almost a century. The delicate pink and white flowers seem to hover over these plants incessantly. Phragmipedium Schroderae is another well know cross with P. caudatum as its other parent. These flowers are large with long, drooping, deep rose petals and last 3 to 4 months.

**Phragmipedium besseae hybrids**: The discovery of P. besseae, with its brilliant orange to red, wide-petaled flowers caused a renewal of interest in phragmipedium hybridizing. The first hybrid to flower was a cross of P. longifolium with P. besseae: Phrag. Mem. Eric Young. The flowers range from salmon to scarlet with outstretched petals like a fiery waxed mustache. Several similar crosses followed; P. Mary Bess: P. besseae x P. caricinum, P. Ecua-Bess: P. besseae x P.ecuadorense. P. Ruby Slippers combined P. caudatum with P. besseae and produced flowers with long drooping petals similar to P. Schroderae, but in salmon to red colors. Two of the most brilliantly colored crosses, P. Mem. Dick Clements and P. Andean Fire, combined P. besseae with P. sargentianum and P. lindleyanum respectively. These two crosses not only display more vibrant colors from the colorful Brazilian species, but have wider, more showy petals, also augmented by these parents. These new crosses have sparked such demand that every possible cross is now being attempted with P. besseae.

**Other new Phragmipediums:** Several other new species have been discovered this decade. Two species very closely allied to P. caricinum and P. pearcei, look like they could easily be hybrids evolved from one or both of these species. These are P. amazonica and P. ecuadoriana. They have been recognized botanically and propagate through seed and vegetative division. Neither are currently common in cultivation, but are rapidly becoming more available. *Phragmipedium hirtzii* was recently discovered in Ecuador. The flowers are somewhat similar to a small P. longifolium, but are a deep brown with the petals angling downward. *Phragmipedium xerophyticum* is tiny, whitish-flowered species out of Mexico, with long rhizomes between the growths. A recent publication has prescribed a new genus for this species: *Mexipedium*, whether or not this genus will remain valid is still questionable.

**Paphiopedilums**

These Asian slipper orchids, have the greatest variety of species and types. Mottled leaf, Brachypetalums: strap leaf multiflorals;

Cochlopetalums, successive blooming, solid green leaf; and Parvisepalums; the Chinese bubble pouch slippers. Due to the large number of species available, many individuals collect only the species. The number of hybrid paphiopedilums is in itself staggering, since paphiopedilums will breed across all sections. The flowers in most of these groups generally last up to three months each. Paphiopedilums are ideal as house plants, requiring only 1500 to 2000 foot candles of light and can easily be grown under lights, even in an office.

**Mottled leaf Paphiopedilums**: This is the largest group of paphiopedilum species and encompasses some 37 species. These plants tend to have a silvery green foliage blotched with darker green. Most are warm to intermediate growing plants, and are generally the first types grown by new paphiopedilums enthusiasts in South Florida. Hybrids in this group will often bloom up to three times a year on large plants and are even used for the cut flower market. One of the more recent trends in breeding of this group was to strive for very dark wine colors known as vinicolors. There has been great success in this endeavor, so that "vinis" are now fairly common. Current trends now combine "vinis" with multifloral as well as complex hybrids.

**Brachypetalums**: "Brachys" are also mottle-leafed, but have rather succulent leaves. These include the species; *P. niveum, P. bellatulum, P. concolor* and *P. godefroyae*. Their flowers are rounded, white or yellow and usually spotted with dark maroon. Brachys are often used in breeding to produce fuller flowers and are found in the background of many of the large, complex, round hybrids. Brachys have been crossed with many of the mottled leaf species to produce very interesting effects. Paphiopedilums Evelyn Rolke (*P. bellatulum x P. sukhakulii*) is a striking example of this line of breeding. This type of cross can be problematic, especially if the mottled leaf parent is used as the pod parent. Since the difference in chromosome number can cause mutations, it is important to pick seedlings that do not exhibit any deformities. Hybrids with solid leaf types have diverged into two directions. Primary and secondary crosses with *P. fairrieanum* produce lovely pastels and stripes like in *P.* Oriental Tapestry and *P.* Tracery. The second line of breeding with solid leaf types is with complex hybrids. Current breeding trends for whites and pinks use large percentages of Brachy blood in their makeup.

**Strap leaf multiflorals**: Multifloral species such as *P. rothschildianum, P. sanderianum, P. philippinense,* and *P. lowii* are some of the most striking of all paphiopedilums. These species produce tall stems of several long-petaled flowers at one time. The plants themselves are often large and impressive. There are just over a dozen species of multiflorals ranging from the giant *P. kolopackingii* with up to 14 flowers per stem and broad leaves with a natural spread of around 3 feet, to the miniature *P. gardeneri* with 2 or 3 dark chestnut flowers on conservative 8-inch leaf span plants.

Many hybrids are made within this group itself, producing glorious stems of flowers in a large range of colors. Best known of these include; *P.* Julius (*P. rothschildianum x P. lowii*), *P.* St. Swithin (*P. rothschildianum x P. philippinense*), *P.* Yellow Tiger (*P. praestans x P. stonei*), and P. Mount Toro *(P. stonei x P. philippinense)*. Newer hybrids using the more uncommon species *P. sanderianum* and *P. kolopackingii* are now becoming very popular. Many of the crosses with *P. sanderianum* have begun to flower, exhibiting very long cascading petals.

Multiflorals have been crossed with all other groups of paphiopedilum. When crossed with mottled leaf types, the result incorporates much of the color pattern of that group. The flower count is reduced since

Paph. Doll Goldi

the mottled leaf types only carry one or two flowers per stem. The use of vinicolor hybrids with multiflorals has produced spectacular hybrids of multiple, long-petaled "vinis." Brachys crossed to multiflorals widen the floral segments and reduce the overall size of the plants. There is also a reduction in flower count due to the reduced flower count of the Brachy parent. Some crosses between the smaller growing multiflorals and brachys bloom more than once a year. These "miniature multiflorals" are ideal for windowsill growing or for any area where space is limited. The most recent multifloral crosses have included those with the Chinese Parvisepalums. This exciting new line of breeding produces crosses with similar petal widening as in the Brachy crosses, but also produces larger, more bubble-like pouches and wonderful colors from the Parvi parents.

**Cochlopetalums:** These are the successive blooming paphiopedilums. The species in this group include *P. primulinum, P. chamberlainianum, P. glaucophyllum,* and *P. victoriamariae.* The individual flowers last for about a month each, but the stem will continue to produce buds for many months. Mature plants stay in flower for 18 months on the same stem. When used in breeding, this characteristic is passed on to the progeny to an extent depending on the percentage of Cochlopetalum parentage.

Paph. Psyche

The most spectacular hybrids are those crosses with the large multiflorals like *P. rothschildianum.* These crosses: P. Transvaal, P. Vanguard, and P. Primchild, produce large colorful long-petaled flowers blooming semi-successively over a 3 to 4 month period. In the case of these three crosses the flowers are very similar in shape, and vary primarily in color as do their Cochlopetalum parents. Crosses have been made with all the multifloral species, and exhibit the common traits of "hairy" edges on the petals as well as the successive flowering characteristic.

Paph. *bellatulum*

Crosses made with Brachypetalums tend to look like slightly narrower petaled forms of their brachy parent, and will bloom successively for up to a year on the same stem.

Crosses with the mottled leaf type are less promising; many tend to be crippled due to incompatibilities in chromosome counts. However, present crosses made with Parvisepalums have been a perfect blend of traits. The progenies tend to look like the

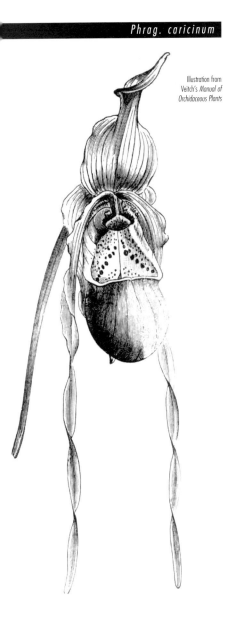

Parvi parent, though somewhat smaller, and produce one flower after another.

**Solid leafed Paphiopedilums**: The species in this group tend to be cooler growing and more difficult to grow in South Florida. Species that have been grown successfully in our area include: *Paphiopedilum. esquerolei, P. spicerianum, P. exul,* and *P. fairrieanum.* Newer species such as *P. henryanum* and *P. tigrinum* are currently being experimented with to see what kind of hybrids will be successful with them. Two of the older species; *P. charlesworthii* and *P. fairrieanum* are also being heavily used to great extent, producing some wonderful new hybrids as well as improved forms of old ones. Paphiopedilum Back Light combines *P. charlesworthii* with a vinicolor P. Red Maude, producing flowers with the *P. charlesworthii* shape and vini coloration.

Complex hybrids have large percentages of this group of species in their background. These hybrid flowers are very large, full and round. Colors include dark reds, whites, pinks, greens, browns, and spotted combinations. The greens, yellow-greens, whites, and pinks seem a little easier to grow in South Florida than the solid reds and spotted flowers. With a little extra care, or indoor culture, this group is being grown successfully in several private collections in our area.

**Parvisepalums**: As with other recently discovered species, Parvisepalums are of great interest to both hobbyist and breeder alike. The five species in this group include; *P. delenatii, P. armeniacum, P. emersonii, P. malipoense* and *P. micranthum.*

Each of these species has the common traits of large bubble like pouches and fairly wide petals. Each species is a different color; pink, yellow, white, green, and striped pink and purplish respectively. They come from areas in China where they get quite cold in the winter, some even flowering through the snow. For this reason some of these species are difficult to flower in South Florida. *Paphiopedilum malipoense* is the easiest to flower, followed by *P. delenatii, P. emersonii, P. armeniacum,* and *P. micranthum* with increasing degrees of difficulty. The hybrids are easier to flower, although care must be taken not to choose crosses between two species that are on the difficult side to flower by themselves, like *P. rothschildianum x P. micranthum*. Although these crosses will eventually bloom in our area, they may take many more years than other crosses.

Crosses between Parvis and the more easily bloomed species flower readily in South Florida. Paphiopedilum Vanda M. Pearman *(P. delenatii x P. bellatulum)* is probably the best known and oldest of Parvi intersectional crosses and blooms very well in our area. Paphiopedilum Gold Dollar *(P. primulinum x P. armeniacum)* blooms easily in a 4" pot and carries the smaller *P. armeniacum* type flowers. Paphiopedilum Ma Belle *(P. malipoense x P. bellatulum)* is currently blooming in 3" pots. Primary crosses of the Parvis such as *P.* Joyce Hasagawa *(P. emersonii x P. delenatii)* and *P.* Magic Lantern *(P. micranthum x P. delenatii)* will also flower on small mature plants.

Slipper orchids are a great addition to any collection. Due to their minimal light requirements they are even ideal for growers who have used up all their greenhouse or outdoor growing space. Just grow them indoors as house plants. And unlike most other orchids, these plants have attractive foliage, so they will still complement a room even when out of bloom.

**Paph. philippinense**

Illustration from Veitch's *Manual of Orchidaceous Plants*

Onc. Sunset Fort

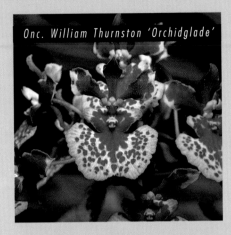

Onc. William Thurnston 'Orchidglade'

Onc. lanceanum X Onc. Mem. Pepita de Restripo

Odm. grande

Onc. splendidum

Brassia maculata

Onc. Sunset Fort

Milt. spectabilis var. mooreliana

Catsetum expansum

Mormodes cartonii

Mormodes sinuatum

Mormodes ignea

# GROWING THE ONCIDIINAE

The Oncidiinae (Oncidium Alliance) consists of a diverse group of New World orchid genera which have more or less similarly shaped flowers with a growth or callus at the base of the lip to attract pollinating insects. They belong to the broad Cymbidium orchid group along with the Maxillarias, Zygopetalinae, and the Stanhoseads.

Initially the Oncidiinae were divided into the major groups of *Oncidium, Odontoglossum* and *Miltonid* on the arbitrary basis of the angle between the lip and the column. Subsequently the *Odontoglossum* and then the *Oncidium* were split into a number of diverse genera. On the basis of molecular biology, the original twenty-six *Oncidium* sections distinguished by Kraenzlin can be combined into seven groups, which may be further reduced to three on the basis of genetic compatibility and chromosome numbers.

The equitant oncidiums, miniature fan-shaped orchids have also been designated as the Variagatum or Rodriguezia group with forty to forty-six chromosomes. Despite their having been considered as the archetype of oncidiums, and accordingly assigned to the section called Oncidium, they have been justifiably removed to the genus *Tolumnia*, genetically compatible with *Comparettia, Rodriguezia, Ionopsis* and *Leochilus*. This group has forty to forty-two chromosomes and its complex hybrids are extremely popular because of their compact growth habit and relatively large, colorful flowers.

The equitant species typically grow at the ends of twigs in low rainfall, but humid Caribbean climates. The hybrids are challenging for the amateur to sustain. They should be grown dry, either plaqued to tree fern or cork, or in small pots with a well draining medium such as a small grade of charcoal or fine grade Aliflor. Plants should be kept in bright light, i.e. vanda light, watered sparingly and fertilized lightly (20-20-20) each week during the warm part of the year. The equitants prefer warm temperatures and good air movement.

The Lophiaris oncidiums might be called the "animal group" since it includes the Mule Ears, the Rat Tails, and the Butterflies. It also includes the non-oncidium genus *Tricocentrium* as well as a few cool growing *Odontoglossum* segregates. While many of the Lophiaris subsections can form primary hybrids, these are usually sterile and cannot serve as the starting point for new breeding lines. These oncidiums have fewer chromosomes, twenty-four to thirty-six, than the main interbreeding groups described later on.

The Mule Ears include species with large thick leaves, e.g. *O. splendidum, O. luridum, O. lanceanum*. They prefer a rapidly draining medium such as Aliflor or various bark or tree-fern mixes and usual cattleya conditions of temperature, light, water, and fertilizing. Larger plants may benefit from basket culture to discourage the interior roots from becoming waterlogged and rotting.

The Butterflies ( twenty-six to thirty-six chromosomes), which are uniquely shaped among the oncidiums, have been transferred to their own genus, *Psychopsis*. This consists of four species, the most available of which are *O. kramerianum* and *O. papilio* (which form the hybrid O. Kalihi). The inflorescences, up to six feet tall, bloom repeatedly over a period of several years and should not be removed unless they die; neither should plants be repotted with active inflorescences.

The Rat Tails (thirty to thirty-six chromosomes) are best grown plaqued and pendant; under cattleya conditions or a bit brighter. The species *O. ascendens, O. cebolleta* and *O. stipitatum* are more easily maintained than the very attractive *O. jonesianum*.

The remaining Oncidiinae, including the genera *Cochlioda, Aspasia, Brassia, Miltonia, Odontoglossum,* and *Ada* interbreed rather freely but vary significantly in temperature tolerance. The cooler growing Pansy Miltonias have been separated from the warm-growing genera. One has to be careful of the claims of warmth tolerance by the commercial hybridizer, they tend to be overly optimistic

## Oncidium maculatum

about the suitability of every hybrid they sell for growing in South Florida.

In general the warmth tolerant oncidium hybrids and the rest of the species with fifty-six to sixty chromosomes, are best grown under typical cattleya conditions of light, water, and fertilizer with a moderately water retentive medium. Although various bark and tree fern mixtures have been used. Reasonable success can be had with a 1:1 mixture of medium grade Aliflor and short fiber sphagnum moss with an underlayer of styrofoam peanuts. Water retentiveness can be increased for seedlings by incorporating higher proportions of sphagnum. Retentiveness may also be adjusted downward for larger plants by increasing Aliflor. Rockwool should not be used because of its tendency to pack down; it also forms a surface slime of algae.

The last remaining genus of Oncidiinae to be considered, *Lockhartia* (fifty-six chromosomes) differs from other Oncidiinae in its braided or dischitous growth habit. Its flower form is typical of Oncidiinae. It has been crossed with the genus *Leochilus*. *Lockhartia* is best grown plaqued under cattleya conditions.

# GROWING TERRESTRIAL ORCHIDS

Phaius tankervilliae

Calanthe Hexham Gem

Habenaria rhodachila

The art of growing orchids terrestrially as garden plants has been practiced in many tropical countries for many years and can easily be done in South Florida.

A selection of tolerant plants are easily obtainable from local nurseries and may be used as natural terrestrials. There are some plants that can be grown terrestially even though they are natural epiphytes.

First prepare the area for growing, use a mix of 2 parts peat, 2 parts bark and 1 part perlite in an area of diffused light, preferably on the south side of trees or the house. Try to mound the bed to allow the best possible drainage. Next plant your orchids. A good first choice is *Phaius tankervilliae* or Nun Orchid. These may be obtained either in bulb form or in 4" or 5" pots; purchase several to make a bed. These plants have leaf spans of 2' or more feet. You should plant them no closer than 2' apart. A bed of 10-12 plants will be spectacular on maturity. Plants planted in early spring should mature and flower from December to February in the same year. Apply a slow release fertilizer since these fast growing plants are heavy

Calanthe rosea

feeders. Being on the ground, they are prone to insect problems such as snails, slugs, grasshoppers, roaches, mice, etc. Frequent light dusting with Sevin powder when they appear seems to keep some of these problems to a minimum.

We have selected the *Phaius* as our primary choice but plants such as *Bletilla, Spathoglottis, Arundina* (Bamboo orchid) *Vanilla,* semi and full terete vandas, and reed stem epidendrums can be grown in very high light even adjusting to full sun. For diffused light, use *Phaius, Thunia, Zygopetalum, Peristeria elata, Sobralia, Phragmipedilum* and cane-type *Dendrobium*. For really sheltered areas, jewel orchids, *Calanthe, Spiranthes, Paphiopedilum* and *Habaneria* seem to do well.

We can only generalize, and some experimenting with light and watering will be needed for optimum results but basically all should follow the same culture.

Protection from cold is a consideration and several options are available. Cover the plants with some type of material that offers frost protection and mulch heavily around the base of the plant. Foliage may be destroyed but the base should reshoot in spring, an alternative is LP infra-red radiant heaters focused on the area you wish to protect. 10,000 - 12, 000 BTU will protect an area of 100 - 150 sq. ft. This choice allows the plants to grow and flower even if the temperature drops to freezing.

It is always a good idea to contact your local orchid society and your local commercial growers for help with any problems you may have. They are always the best sources for local growing information.

# GROWING THE CATASETINAE

Illustration from
Veitch's *Manual of
Orchidaceous Plants*

The Catasetinae (Catasetum Alliance) consist of some of the most beautiful, fragrant and unusual orchids known. They include several interfertile genera: *Catasetum, Cycnoches* and *Mormodes*. Recently two additional genera have been split from Catasetum, namely *Clowesia* and *Dressleria*. The Catasetinae are distantly related to other genera of the Cymbidium tribe, including *Gramatophyllum, Stanhopea, Maxillaria* and *Oncidium*.

The most distinctive features of the Catasetinae arise from the strategies they have evolved for preventing self-pollination. In contrast to the bisexual flowers of most orchids, catasetum flowers are unisexual, either male or female, each with its own flower form. Historically, this caused no end of confusion in identifying the different sex-related forms of the same species, compounded by the fact that from time to time the same plant can bear flowers of different sexes. In general, the rarer female flowers are borne on the most vigorously growing plants, i.e. larger pseudo-bulbs and higher light intensities. Male catasetum flowers are spectacular in their ability to eject pollinia several feet when the trigger hairs on the column are touched (look out bees!)

In most of the Central American catasetums the lip is hooded (e.g. *C. maculatum, C. verdiflavin*) while the lips of the South American male catasetum flowers tend to be flat and broad (*C. pilateum, C. fimbriatum*).

Formerly the genus *Catasetum* included all Catasetinae which flowered from the base of their pseudobulbs. One subgroup, which features bisexual, thin flowers with a minty

Illustration from Veitch's *Manual of Orchidaceous Plants*

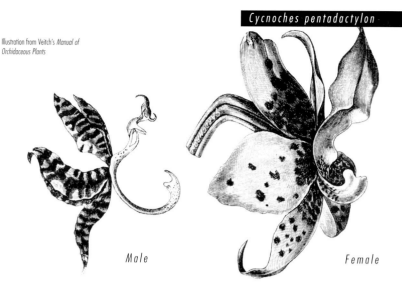

Male                    Female

fragrance has been transferred to the genus *Clowesia*. Another subgroup with fleshy bisexual flowers has been transferred to *Dressleria*.

The inflorescences of the remaining Catasetinae genera arise from the upper nodes of the pseudobulbs. The *Cynoches* or swan neck orchids take their name from the graceful arch of the column. In the Eucycnoches subgroup (e.g. *C. chlorochilon*) male and female flowers are similar. In the Heteranthe subgroup (e.g. *C. ergertonianum*) the male flowers are much smaller and hang down in dense racemes.

Mormodes flowers (e.g. *M. buccunator*) known as the Goblin orchids, are bisexual and distinguished by a twisted lip and column which must vex orchid judges with rigid standards of symmetry. Fresh flowers are functionally male since access of bees to the stigma is blocked. Only after visiting bees remove the pollinaria does the column slowly untwist and permit subsequent visitors to deposit pollinia stuck to their bodies onto the stigma.

Although the genus *Galeandra* is not usually considered within the Catasetinae its

affinity to them is confirmed by its ability to hybridize with *Catasetum*. It has elongated cane-like pseudobulbs with successively blooming upper node inflorescences. This genus should be grown a bit dryer in a basket but otherwise under the same seasonal treatment as the Catasetinae.

The Catasetinae, both species and hybrids, are grown in deep slotted pots with a medium of short fiber sphagnum moss underlayed with styrofoam peanuts. During their period of active growth (April - October) water heavily and keep the medium moist at all times and fertilize weekly with 20-20-20. Catasetinae thrive in bright light, tolerating full sun for at least part of the day, although they will bloom reasonably well in cattleya light. Each mature plant blooms 2-3 times a season.

Around November growth stops and leaves start to wither, although some Catasetinae continue to bloom throughout the month. As each plant loses its leaves and finishes blooming, it

Galeandra baurii

Ctsm. Susan Fuchs

Ctsm. Orchidglade

should be moved to a location where it receives only rainfall until spring. The combination which is deadly for Catasetinae is cold and wet. However if they are wintered too dry the pseudobulbs shrivel and also become susceptible to rot. If at the end of December some leaves remain, they are removed to assure dormancy. Dry, and in their old pots, Catasetinae will tolerate short spells of cold, as low as 38 °F. Below this temperature it might be prudent to move dormant plants to warmer conditions.

In March, signs of new growth appear at the base of some of the pseudobulbs. At this time those orchids breaking dormancy are removed from their pots and trimmed of all roots, which by now are dead. If any pseudobulbs have rotted, they are cut out, even if this divides the clump. Divide any clump with five or more pseudobulbs.

The cleaned plants or divisions are inserted ($^3/_4$ inch) into fresh sphagnum moss underlayed with styrofoam peanuts in clean pots, and supported by rings and are returned to their previous well-watered location. After allowing two to three weeks for the plant to grow roots, a generous dose of 14-14-14 Osmocoat is added to each pot which completes the annual growth cycle. If any plants have failed to show growth by the end of March, or first two weeks of April, they are treated as if they had shown new growth.

Ctsm. piliatum

# FLORIDA ORCHIDS

As orchid enthusiasts we are very fortunate to live in Florida. Not only is the climate ideal for cultivating many species and hybrids of orchids but we have over 100 species of orchids growing naturally in Florida. On almost any day within a few minutes drive from our homes we can observe many species of orchids flowering in the wild.

Just a few years ago we could find thousands of *Encyclia tampensis* growing at the base of cabbage palmettos in the pinelands in southern Dade County. *Bletia purpurea, Spiranthes torta, Habenaria quinqueseta, Habenaria floribunda* and *Eulophia alta* were all very common in the pinelands and along the roadsides. Unfortunately they are almost all gone now. However, we still can find an occasional *E. tampensis* and *B. purpurea* in some of the small pockets of pinelands that have survived. In the spring *Spiranthes vernalis* can be found along the roadsides if they have not been recently mowed. The grassy shoulders of the Turnpike Extension starting in Florida City are a host to thousands of *S. vernalis*. At times there are so many plants that they appear as white patches. *Triphora gentianoides* is also found commonly in back yards along with two imports which have

*Platanthera blephaglottis*

*Onc. floridanum*

*Platanthera ciliaris*

*cradenia lutescens*

become naturalized, *Oeceoclades maculata* and *Zeuxine strateumatica*. *Oeceoclades maculata* was brought to Florida and cultivated at Fairchild Tropical Garden from where it escaped. The reproductive history of this plant was not known at the time, but later it was found out that it self-pollinates and can grow from seed to flowering in one year. This is an amazing orchid which can grow in almost any habitat from the deepest shade to full sun. The other import which now can be found in every county of Florida, *Z. strateumatica*, was first imported into the United States with grass seeds from China.

Although historically nearly 50 species were known to occur in what are now the populated areas of Dade County and Broward County just the few species mentioned above have survived the extensive habitat destruction. However, all of the species that have been known to occur in South Florida still can be found in the Everglades National Park with the exception of *Brassia caudata*. Until recently it was believed that both *B. caudata* and *Macradenia lutescens* were extinct from South Florida due to a combination of illegal collecting and habitat destruc-

tion by natural forces. *Macradenia lutescens* was just discovered in a remote hammock several miles from where it was originally found. Although *B. caudata* was not seen it may still be discovered in the same area.

In early spring only a short ride south into the Everglades National Park many species of orchids can be seen flowering along the roadside. A sharp eye is necessary to see most of the species since they tend to blend in with the other roadside flowers common at that time of the year. In the wet ditches and along the rocky edges of the pinelands the following species can be observed in flower: *Bletia purpurea, Habenaria floribunda* (syn. *Habenaria odontopetala*), *Habenaria quinqueseta, Habenaria repens, Mesadenus polyanthus, Platanthera nivea, Spiranthes praecox, Spiranthes torta, Spiranthes vernalis* and *Zeuxine strateumatica*.

Growing in cracks in rocks and soil pockets in the pinelands can be found: *Basiphyllaea corallicola* and *Ponthieva brittoniae*. Both of these species are found in large colonies but few colonies have been located.

In the hardwood hammocks can be observed the following species growing epiphytically or terrestrially: *Anacheilium cochleatum* var. *triandrum*, *Beadlea elata*, *Beloglottis costaricensis*, *Cranichis muscosa*, *Prescotia oligantha*, *Eltroplectris calcarata*, *Encyclia tampensis*, *Epidendrum anceps*, *Epidendrum nocturnum*, *Epidendrum rigidum*, *Galeandra beyrichii*, *Govenia utriculata*, *Ionopsis utricularioides*, *Liparis elata*, *Beadlea cranichoides*, *Macradenia lutescens*, *Malaxis spicata*, *Oeceoclades maculata*, *Oncidium floridanum* (usually growing lithophytically), *Pelexia adnata*, *Platythelys querceticola*, *Polystachya concreta*, *Triphora gentianoides*, *Vanilla mexicana* (syn. *Vanilla planifolia*) *and Vanilla phaeantha*.

In open grassy wet praries or open depressions in the pinelands the following can be found: *Calopogon multiflorus*, *Calopogon tuberosus*, *Eulophia alta*, *Spiranthes odorata*, *Stenorrhynchus lanceolatus* var. *lanceolatus* and *Stenorrhynchus lanceolatus* var. *luteoalba*.

Growing epiphytically on cypress trees in the open cypress country are found: *Encyclia tampensis* and *Cyrtopodium punctatum*.

Many of the above epiphytes also grow along the mangrove and buttonwood lined creeks and rivers which penetrate deep inland into South Florida. If some of the creeks and rivers in Seven Palm Lake, Hell's Bay, Whitewater Bay, Lostman's River and Turner River areas are explored the following orchids can also be observed: *Campylocentrum pachyrrhizum*, *Epicladium boothianum* var. *erythronioides* (syn. *Encyclia boothiana* var. *erythronioides*), *Epidendrum floridense* (The epithet *difforme* has been incorrectly applied to the Florida populations), *Harrisella porrecta*, *Oncidium undulatum* (This species was incorrectly identified as *Oncidium luridum*, a Central American species), *Polyrrhisa lindenii* and *Vanilla barbellata*.

Many of the rarer species can only

be found deep into the interior parts of the park.

With a shallow draft boat a very exciting and rewarding excursion can be made from the Flamingo Marina to Chokoloskee Island. The trip is approximately 100 miles one way through some of the most unique and beautiful country in the world. The ride can be made from Flamingo to Chokoloskee and back in one day, but it would be best to stay overnight in Chokoloskee.

The trip is best made at a slow pace in order to fully enjoy the orchids and animal life. An early morning start in the Buttonwood canal which joins

Polyrrhiza lindenii

Encyclia tampensis

Encyclia tampensis

Flamingo with Coot Bay will be rewarded by the animal life which can be seen. Along the canal and sometimes overhanging the canal can be seen hundreds of *Encyclia tampensis* in flower during the summer. *Oncidium undulatum, Epicladium boothianum* var. *erythronioides, Epidendrum floridense, Polystachya concreta* and *Vanilla barbellata* can be found abundantly along the east side of the canal growing epiphytically in the mangroves and buttonwoods. These same species can be found along the rest of the Wilderness Waterway. The mangroves along the Shark River, Harney River, Broad River and the many narrow creeks joining the large bays are especially productive to observe orchids. Short trips off the Wilderness Waterway into Hell's Bay, Robert's River and North River can be very interesting. An interesting trip is from Shark River into Tarpon Bay, through Avocado Creek past Canepatch into either Squawk Creek or Rookery Branch. These creeks are so far inland that they become fresh water and many species of orchids and bromeliads are found.

Just northeast of the Everglades National Park is the Fakahatchee Strand. This is a spectacular slew with many species of orchids not found anywhere else in Florida. *Bulbophyllum pachyrhachis* and

Calopogon tuberosus

*Epidendrum blancheanum* were once found there but are now believed to be extinct due to illegal collecting. *Hormidium pygmaeum, Lepanthopsis melanantha, Maxillaria crassifolia, Epidendrum strobiliferum* and *Pleurothallis gelida* although rare can still be occasionally found.

Martin county is known for two species not found anywhere else in Florida, *Tolumnia bahamensis* growing in the white sand scrub and *Vanilla inodora* growing in palmettos in coastal hammocks.

With the exception of *Encyclia tampensis* which is found as far north as Citrus county the only epiphytic orchid found in central and northern Florida is *Epidendrum conopsum*. It is found to be abundant growing on large oak trees. However, central and northern Florida is extremely rich in many species of beautiful terrestrial orchids. Most of these orchids are underground for the majority of the year. In the spring or late summer these species produce flower spikes, flower, set seed pods and die back, repeating the cycle the following year.

In late summer many roadsides in northern Florida come into flower with thousands of orchids. *Platanthera blephariglottis* var. *conspicua, Platanthera ciliaris, Platanthera clavellata, Platanthera cristata, Platanthera flava, Platanthera integra* and the natural hybrids: *Platanthera xbicolor, Platanthera xcanbyi* and *Platanthera xchapmanii* become roadside weeds in the ditches along roads and at the edges of pinelands. In the spring the calopogons and spiranthes adorn the roadsides. *Calopogon pallidus, Calopogon barbatus, Calopogon multiflorus* and *Calopogon tuberosus* are very common along with *Pogonia ophioglossoides* and *Ponthieva racemosa*. In central Florida *Habenaria distans, Hexalectris spicata, Pteroglossaspis ecristata, Listera australis, Malasis unifolia, Cleistes divaricata, Corallorrhiza odontorhiza, Corallorrhiza wisteriana, Spiranthes brevilabris, Spiranthes brevilabris* var. *floridana, Spiranthes cernua, Spiranthes lacera* var. *gracilis, Spiranthes laciniata, Spiranthes longilabris* and *Spiranthes tuberosa* can be found along roadsides and in a variety of habitats. In extreme northern Florida are found *Goodyear pubescens, Isotria verticillata* and *Tipularia discolor*. In a very small isolated habitat near Brooksville are found four rare orchids: *Triphora craigheadii, Triphora latifolia, Triphora trianthophoros* and *Triphora yucatanensis*.

It is extremely important to remember that collecting of any plants is strictly prohibited by law and can result in stiff penalties and confiscation of property. It must be emphasized that by only observing the orchids in their natural habitat they will be there for us and for future generations to enjoy every year. Although the water levels have changed in South Florida due to mismanagement of resources, the orchids are adapting and their numbers are increasing and will continue to do so if they are not collected.

**Encyclia boothiana var.**

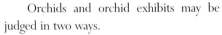

# AOS Orchids Judging

Orchids and orchid exhibits may be judged in two ways.

In one type of judging, orchid plants and cut flowers, either singly or in groups, compete within classes defined by the show schedule for first, second, and third place prize for each class. This is called show judging, also called ribbon judging, since blue, red and white ribbons are commonly used to designate first, second or third place.

In the other type of judging, orchid plants or cut flowers, usually singly but occasionally in groups, are evaluated for their intrinsic merit against a hypothetical standard of perfection in the mind of each judge. This is called award or merit judging since worthy plants or exhibits are granted specific awards in recognition of their intrinsic merits.

Awards that may be granted are:

- Educational Exhibit Certificates:
  Awarded to an educational exhibit that scores at least 90 points.

- Certificate of Meritorious Arrangement:
  Awarded to an outstanding exhibit in the flower arrangement class of a show in which orchid flowers are dominant.

- Artistic Certificate (for Artistic Display of Orchids in Use):
  Awarded to an outstanding exhibit of not less than 25 square feet which the judges consider to be exceptionally artistic.

### Flower Awards:

- First Class Certificate (FCC):
  Awarded to an orchid species or hybrid which scores 90 points or more.

- Award of Merit (AM):
    Awarded to an orchid species or hybrid which scores between 80 and 89 points.

- Highly Commended Certificate (HCC):
    Awarded to an orchid species or hybrid which scores between 75 and 79 points.

### Judges Commendation (JC):
    Awarded to flowers or plants, individually or in groups, which in the opinion of the judges, have specific values, but they are unable to score.

- Award of Distinction (AD):
    Awarded once to a cross, exhibited individually or collectively, representing a worthy new direction in breeding.

- Award of Quality (AQ):
    Awarded once to a cross, exhibited by a single individual as a group of not less than 12 different clones or the inflorescences thereof, of a raised species or hybrid when the result is a sufficient improvement over the former type. One or more cultivars exhibited must receive, or have received, a flower quality award.

- Certificate of Cultural Merit (CCM):
    Awarded to the exhibitor of a specimen plant of robust health and appearance with an unusually large number of flowers. Must score at least 80 points and must have been in the care of the exhibitor at least six months immediately prior to the award.

- Certificate of Horticultural Merit (CHM):
    Awarded to a cultivar of a well-grown and well-flowered species or natural hybrid outstanding esthetic appeal that contributes to the horticultural aspects of orchidology. Must score at least 80 points and the entire plant must be exhibited.

- Certificate of Botanical Recognition (CBR):

Awarded to a cultivar of a species or natural hybrid deemed worthy of recognition for rarity, novelty, and educational value. The entire plant must be exhibited and no award of any kind may have previously been made to the species as a taxon. No point score is used but the award shall be granted only by the affirmative vote of at least two-thirds of the judging team assigned.

*Information from the American Orchid Society's Handbook on Judging and Exhibition Eighth Edition.*

## THE AMERICAN ORCHID SOCIETY

The American Orchid Society, Inc., a non-profit, educational, scientific and horticultural organization, is the world's largest society devoted exclusively to orchids. The Society's primary purposes are to disseminate knowledge of all phases of orchidology, to encourage scientific research on orchids and to stimulate the growing, hybridizing and use of orchids. To help achieve these objectives, the Society publishes a monthly magazine, *Orchids*, which goes to all the members. A subscription to this publication is included in the annual dues.

Through it's panel of certified judges, the Society grants awards for fine flowers and provides show trophies for meritorious orchid exhibits.

Society headquarters are located at 6000 South Olive Avenue, West Palm Beach, Florida 33405.

# ORCHID NAMES

Abbreviations followed by * are not officially recognized by the RHS. These are genera that have won AOS awards, but have not been used in hybridization and therefore do not have an official RHS abbreviation. These abbreviations were generated by using the first letter of the Genus name, then using the first 5 consonants (if appropriate) to achieve a 6 letter abbreviation.

| GENUS | ABBREV | FORMULA |
|---|---|---|
| Acacallis | Acclls* | Natural |
| Acampe | Acp | Natural |
| Acinbreea | Acba | Acn x Emb |
| Acineta | Acn | Natural |
| Ada | Ada | Natural |
| Adacidium | Adcm | Ada x Onc |
| Adaglossum | Adgm | Ada x Odm |
| Adioda | Ado | Ada x Cda |
| Aerangis | Aergs | Natural |
| Aeranthes | Aerth | Natural |
| Aerasconetia | Aescta | Aer x Asctm x Neof |
| Aeridachnis | Aerdns | Aer x Arach |
| Aerides | Aer | Natural |
| Aeridisia | Aersa | Aer x Lsa |
| Aeriditis | Aerdts | Aer x Dor |
| Aeridocentrum | Aerctm | Aer x Asctm |
| Aeridochilus | Aerchs | Aer x Sarco |
| Aeridofinetia | Aerf | Aer x Neof |
| Aeridoglossum | Aergm | Aer x Ascgm |
| Aeridoglottis | Aegts | Aer x Trgl |
| Aeridopsis | Aerps | Aer x Phal |
| Aeridovanda | Aerdv | Aer x V |
| Aeridovanisia | Aervsa | Aer x Lsa x V |
| Aganisia | Agn | Natural |
| Aitkenara | Aitk | Otst x Z x Zspm |
| Alangreatwoodara | Agwa | Clx x Prom x A |
| Alexanderara | Alxra | Brs x Cda x Odm x Onc |
| Aliceara | Alcra | Brs x Milt x Onc |
| Allenara | Alna | C x Diacm x Epi x L |
| Alphonsoara | Alph | Arach x Asctm x V x Vdps |
| Ambostoma | Amb | Natural |
| Andrewara | Andw | Arach x Ren x Trgl x V |

| GENUS | ABBREV | FORMULA |
|---|---|---|
| Angraecentrum | Angctm | Angcm x Asctm |
| Angraecostylis | Angsts | Angcm x Rhy |
| Angraecum | Angcm | Natural |
| Angraecyrtanthes | Ancyth | Aerth x Angcm X Cyrtcs |
| Angraeorchis | Angchs | Angcm x Cyrtcs |
| Angrangis | Angrs | Aergs x Angcm |
| Angranthellea | Angtla | Aerth x Angcm x Jum |
| Angranthes | Angth | Aerth x Angcm |
| Angreoniella | Angnla | Angcm x Oenla |
| Anguloa | Ang | Natural |
| Angulocaste | Angcst | Ang x Lyc |
| Anoectochilus | Anct | Natural |
| Anoectomaria | Anctma | Anct x Haem |
| Ansellia | Aslla | Natural |
| Ansieium | Asdm | Aslla x Cym |
| Aracampe | Arcp | Acp x Arach |
| Arachnanthe | Archnn* | Natural |
| Arachnis | Arach | Natural |
| Arachnoglossum | Arngm | Arach x Ascgm |
| Arachnoglottis | Arngl | Arach x Trgl |
| Arachnopsis | Arnps | Arach x Phal |
| Arachnostylis | Arnst | Arach x Rhy |
| Aranda | Aranda | Arach x V |
| Aranthera | Arnth | Arach x Ren |
| Arethusa | Aret | Natural |
| Arizara | Ariz | C x Dga x Epi |
| Armodorum | Armdrm* | Natural |
| Arundina | | |
| Ascandopsis | Ascdps | Asctm x Vdps |
| Ascocenda | Ascda | Asctm x V |
| Ascocentrum | Asctm | Natural |
| Ascocleinetia | Ascln | Asctm x Clctn x Neof |
| Ascofinetia | Ascf | Asctm x Neof |
| Ascogastisia | Agsta | Asctm x Gchls x Lsa |
| Ascoglossum | Ascgm | Natural |
| Ascoglottis | Asgts | Asctm x Trgl |
| Asconopsis | Ascps | Asctm x Phal |
| Ascorachnis | Ascns | Arach x Asctm |
| Ascovandoritis | Asvts | Asctm x Dor x V |
| Aspasia | Asp | Natural |
| Aspasium | Aspsm | Asp x Onc |
| Aspodia | Asid | Asp x Cda |
| Aspodonia | Aspd | Asp x Milt x Odm |
| Aspoglossum | Aspgm | Asp x Odm |
| Ayubara | Ayb | Aer x Arach x Ascgm |
| Bakerara | Bak | Brs x Milt x Odm x Onc |

| | | |
|---|---|---|
| Baldwinara | Bdwna | Asp x Cda x Odm x Onc |
| Banfieldara | Bnfd | Ada x Brs x Odm |
| Barangis | Brgs | Aergs x Brmb |
| Baptirettia | Btta | Bapt x Comp |
| Baptistonia | Bapt | Natural |
| Barbosaara | Bbra | Cda x Gom x Odm x Onc |
| Barombia | Brmb | Natural |
| Bardendrum | Bard | Bark x Epi |
| Barkeria | Bark | Natural |
| Barkonitis | Bknts | Bark x Soph |
| Batemannia | Btmna | Natural |
| Bateostylis | Btst | Btmna x Otst |
| Baumannara | Bmnra | Comp x Odm x Onc |
| Beallara | Bllra | Brs x Cda x Milt x odm |
| Beardara | Bdra | Asctm x Dor x Phal |
| Bifrenaria | Bif | Natural |
| Bifrenidium | Bifdm | Bif x Zwr |
| Bifreniella | Bifla | Bif x Rud |
| Bishopara | Bish | Bro x C x Soph |
| Blackara | Blkr | Asp x Cda x Milt x Odm |
| Blephariglottis | Blphrg* | Natural |
| Bletia | Bletia | Natural |
| Bletilla | Ble | Natural |
| Bloomara | Blma | Bro x Lps x Ttma |
| Bokchoonara | Bkch | Arach x Asctm x Phal x V |
| Bollea | Bol | Natural |
| Bollopetalum | Blptm | Bol x Z |
| Bovornara | Bov | Arach x Asctm x Rhy x V |
| Bradeara | Brade | Comp x Gom x Rdza |
| Brapasia | Brap | Asp x Brs |
| Brassada | Brsa | Ada x Brs |
| Brassavola | B | Natural |
| Brassia | Brs | Natural |
| Brassidium | Brsdm | Brs x Onc |
| Brassioda | Broda | Brs x Cda |
| Brassocattleya | Bc | B x C |
| Brassochilus | Brchs | Brs x Lchs |
| Brassodiacrium | Bdia | B x Diacm |
| Brassoepidendrum | Bepi | B x Epi |
| Brassoepilaelia | Bpl | B x Epi x L |
| Brassokeria | Brsk | Bark x B |
| Brassolaelia | Bl | B x L |
| Brassolaeliocattleya | Blc | B x C x L |
| Brassosophronitis | Bnts | B x Soph |
| Brassotonia | Bstna | B x Bro |
| Brilliandeara | Brlda | Asp x Brs x Cda x Milt x Odm x Onc |
| Broughtonia | Bro | Natural |
| Brownara | Bwna | Bro x C x Diacm |
| Brummittara | Brum | Comp x Odm x Rdza |
| Buiara | Bui | Bro x C x Epi x L x Soph |
| Bulbophyllum | Bulb | Natural |
| Burkhardtara | Bktra | Lchs x Odm x Onc x Rdza |
| Burkillara | Burk | Aer x Arach x V |
| Burrageara | Burr | Cda x Milt x Odm x Onc |
| Caladenia | Calda | Natural |
| Calanthe | Cal | Natural |
| Caloarethusa | Clts | Aret x Cpg |
| Calopogon | Cpg | Natural |
| Campbellara | Cmpba | Odm x Onc x Rdza |
| Carpenterara | Cptra | Bapt x Odm x Onc |
| Carterara | Ctra | Aer x Ren x Vdps |
| Casoara | Csr | B x Bro x Lps |
| Catamodes | Ctmds | Ctsm x Morm |
| Catanoches | Ctnchs | Ctsm x Cyc |
| Catasandra | Ctsda | Ctsm x Gal |
| Catasetum | Ctsm | Natural |
| Cattkeria | Cka | Bark x C |
| Cattleya | C | Natural |
| Cattleyopsis | Ctps | Natural |
| Cattleyopsisgoa | Ctpga | Ctps x Dga |
| Cattleyopsistonia | Ctpsta | Bro x Ctps |
| Cattleytonia | Ctna | Bro x C |
| Cattotes | Ctts | C x Lpt |
| Caularthron | Clrthr* | Natural |
| Charlesworthara | Cha | Cda x Milt x Onc |
| Charlieara | Charl | Rhy x V x Vdps |
| Chewara | Chew | Aer x Ren x Rhy |
| Chilocentrum | Chctm | Asctm x Chsch |
| Chiloschista | Chsch | Natural |
| Chondrobollea | Chdb | Bol x Chdrh |
| Chondrorhyncha | Chdrh | Natural |
| Christieara | Chtra | Aer x Asctm x V |
| Chuanyenara | Chnya | Arach x Ren x Rhy |
| Chyletia | Chlt | Natural |
| Chysis | Chy | Natural |
| Cirrhopetalum | Cirr | Natural |
| Cirrhophyllum | Crphm | Bulb x Cirr |
| Cischostalix | Cstx | Cisch x Sgmx |
| Cischweinfia | Cisch | Natural |
| Cleisocalpa | Clclp | Clctn x Pmcpa |

| | | | | | |
|---|---|---|---|---|---|
| Cleisocentron | Clctn | Natural | Diacattleya | Diaca | C x Diacm |
| Cleisodes | Clsd | Aer x Clctn | Diacrium | Diacm | Natural |
| Cleisofinetia | Clfta | Clctn x Neof | Diakeria | Dkra | Bark x Diacm |
| Cleisonopsis | Clnps | Clctn x Phal | Dialaelia | Dial | Diacm x L |
| Cleisopera | Clspa | Cleis x Micr | Dialaeliocattleya | Dialc | C x Diacm x L |
| Cleisoquetia | Clq | Clctn x Rbq | Dialaeliopsis | Dialps | Diacm x Lps |
| Cleisostoma | Cleis | Natural | Diaphanangis | Dpgs | Aergs x Dpthe |
| Cleisostylis | Clsty | Clctn x Rhy | Diaphananthe | Dpthe | Natural |
| Cleisothera | Cltha | Cleis x Pthia | Dieselara | Dsla | L x Schom x Soph |
| Clowesia | Clow | Natural | Dillonara | Dill | Epi x L x Schom |
| Cochella | Chla | Cnths x Mdcla | Diplonopsis | Dpnps | Dpra x Phal |
| Cochleanthes | Cnths | Natural | Diploprora | Dpra | Natural |
| Cochlecaste | Cccst | Cnths x Lyc | Disa | Disa | Natural |
| Cochlenia | Cclna | Snths x Stenia | Diuris | Diuris | Natural |
| Cochleottia | Colta | Cnths x Glta | Domindesmia | Ddma | Dga x Hex |
| Cochlepetalum | Ccptm | Cnths x Z | Domingoa | Dga | Natural |
| Cochlioda | Cda | Natural | Domintonia | Dmtna | Bro x Dga |
| Colaste | Cste | Clx x Lyc | Dominyara | Dmya | Asctm x Lsa x Neof x Rhy |
| Colax | Clx | Natural | | | |
| Colmanara | Colm | Milt x Odm x Onc | Domliopsis | Dmlps | Dga x Lps |
| Comparettia | Comp | Natural | Doncollinara | Dclna | Cda x Odm x Rdza |
| Conphronitis | Conph | Const x Soph | Dorandopsis | Ddps | Dor x Vdps |
| Constantia | Const | Natural | Doricentrum | Dctm | Asctm x Dor |
| Cookara | Cook | Bro x C x Diacm x L | Doriella | Drlla | Dor x King |
| Coryanthes | Crths | Natural | Doriellaopsis | Dllps | Dor x King x Phal |
| Coryhopea | Crhpa | Crths x Stan | Dorifinetia | Dfta | Dor x Neof |
| Crawwhayara | Craw | Asp x Brs x Milt x Onc | Doriglossum | Drgm | Ascgm x Dor |
| Cryptopus | Crypt | Natural | Doristylis | Dst | Dor x Rhy |
| Cycnoches | Cyc | Natural | Doritaenopsis | Dtps | Dor x Phal |
| Cycnodes | Cycd | Cyc x Morm | Doritis | Dor | Natural |
| Cymbidiella | Cymla | Natural | Dorthera | Dtha | Dor x Ren |
| Cymbidium | Cym | Natural | Dossinia | Doss | Natural |
| Cymphiella | Cymph | Cym x Eul | Dossinimaria | Dsma | Doss x Haem |
| Cynorkis | Cyn | Natural | Downsara | Dwsa | Agn x Btmna x Otst x Zspm |
| Cyperorchis | Cporch | Natural | | | |
| Cypripedium | Cyp | Natural | Dracula | Drac | Natural |
| Cyrtellia | Cyrtl | Aslla x Cyrt | Dracuvallia | Drvla | Drac x Masd |
| Cyrtochilum | Cyrtch* | Natural | Dresslerara | Dres | Ascgm x Phal x Ren |
| Cyrtopodium | Cyrt | Natural | Drymoanthus | Dry | Natural |
| Cyrtorchis | Cyrtcs | Natural | Duggerara | Dugg | Ada x Brs x Milt |
| Dactylorhiza | Dact | Natural | Dunnara | Dnna | Bro x Ctps x Dga |
| Darwinara | Dar | Asctm x Neof x Rhy x V | Dunningara | Dngra | Asp x Milt x Onc |
| | | | Durutyara | Dtya | Btmna x Osts x Z x Zspm |
| Debruyneara | Dbra | Asctm x Lsa x V | | | |
| Degarmoara | Dgmra | Brs x Milt x Odm | Eastonara | Eas | Asctm x Gchls x V |
| Dekensara | Dek | B x C x Schom | Edeara | Edr | Arach x Phal x Ren x Vdps |
| Dendrobium | Den | Natural | | | |
| Dendroberia | Denga | Den x Flkga | Embreea | Emb | Natural |
| Devereuxara | Dvra | Asctm x Phal x V | Encyclia | Encycl* | Natural |
| Diabroughtonia | Diab | Bro x Diacm | Ephemerantha | Ephem | Natural |

| Epibarkiella | Epbkl | Bark x Epi x Ngl |
|---|---|---|
| Epibrassonitis | Epbns | B x Epi x Soph |
| Epicatonia | Epctn | Bro x C x Epi |
| Epicattleya | Epc | C x Epi |
| Epidella | Epdla | Epi x Ngl |
| Epidendrum | Epi | Natural |
| Epidiacrium | Epdcm | Diacm x Epi |
| Epigolttis | Epgl | Epi x Scgl |
| Epigoa | Epg | Dga x Epi |
| Epilaelia | Epl | Epi x L |
| Epilaeliocattleya | Eplc | C x Epi x L |
| Epilaeliopsis | Eplps | Epi x Lps |
| Epiopsis | Eps | Ctps x Epi |
| Epipactis | Epcts | Natural |
| Epiphronitis | Ephs | Epi x Soph |
| Epistoma | Epstm | Amb x Epi |
| Epitonia | Eptn | Bro x Epi |
| Ernestara | Entra | Phal x Ren x Vdps |
| Erycina | Ercn | Natural |
| Eryidium | Erdm | Ercn x Onc |
| Esmeralda | Esmrls* | Natural |
| Euanthe | Enth* | Natural |
| Eulocymbidiella | Eucmla | Cymla x Eul |
| Eulophia | Eupha | Natural |
| Eulophiella | Eul | Natual |
| Euryangis | Eugs | Aergs x Echn |
| Eurychone | Echn | Natural |
| Eurygraecum | Eugcm | Angcm x Echn |
| Eurynopsis | Eunps | Echn x Phal |
| Freedara | Frda | Ascgm x Ren x Vdps |
| Fergusonara | Ferg | B x C x L x Schom x Soph |
| Fialaara | Fia | Bro x C x L x Lps |
| Flickingeria | Flkga | Natural |
| Forgetara | Fgtra | Asp x Brs x Milt |
| Fujioara | Fjo | Asctm x Trgl x V |
| Fujiwarara | Fjw | B x C x Lps |
| Galeandra | Gal | Natural |
| Galeansellia | Gslla | Aslla x Gal |
| Galeopetalum | Gptm | Gtla x Z |
| Galeosepalum | Glspm | Glta x Zspm |
| Galeottia | Glta | Natural |
| Gastisia | Gsta | Gchls x Lsa |
| Gastisocalpa | Gscpa | Gchls x Lsa x Pmcpa |
| Gastritis | Gtts | Dor x Gchls |
| Gastrochiloglottis | Gchgl | Gchls x Trgl |
| Gastrochilus | Gchls | Natural |
| Gastrosarcochilus | Gsarco | Gchls x Sarco |
| Gastrothera | Gsrth | Gchls x Ren |
| Gauntlettara | Gtra | Bro x Ctps x Lps |
| Georgeblackara | Gbka | Comp x Lchs x Onc x Rdza |
| Goffara | Gfa | Lsa x Rhy x V |
| Gohartia | Ghta | Gom x Lhta |
| Gomada | Gmda | Ada x Gom |
| Gomesa | Gom | Natural |
| Gomettia | Gmtta | Comp x Gom |
| Gomochilus | Gmch | Gom x Lchs |
| Gomoglossum | Gmgm | Gom x Odm |
| Gongora | Gga | Natural |
| Goodaleara | Gdlra | Brs x Cda x Milt x Odm x Onc |
| Gottererara | Gott | Asctm x Ren x Vdps |
| Grammatocymbidium | Grcym | Cym x Gram |
| Grammatophyllum | Gram | Natural |
| Grammatopodium | Grtp | Cyrt x Gram |
| Graphiella | Grpla | Cymla Grks |
| Graphorkis | Grks | Natural |
| Habenaria | Hab | Natural |
| Hagerara | Hgra | Dor x Phal x V |
| Haemaria | Haem | Natural |
| Hamelwellsara | Hmwsa | Agn x Btmna x Otst x Z x Zspm |
| Hanesara | Han | Aer x Arach x Neof |
| Hartara | Hart | Bro x L x Soph |
| Hasegawaara | Hasgw | B x Bro x C x L x Soph |
| Hattoriara | Hatt | B x Bro x C x Epi x L |
| Hausermannara | Haus | Dor x Phal x Vdps |
| Hawaiiara | Haw | Ren x V x Vdps |
| Hawkesara | Hwkra | C x Ctps x Epi |
| Hawkinsara | Hknsa | Bro x C x L x Soph |
| Helcia | Hlc | Natural |
| Helpilia | Hpla | Hlc x Trpla |
| Herbertara | Hbtr | C x L x Schom x Soph |
| Hexadesmia | Hex | Natural |
| Hexisea | Hxsa | Natural |
| Higashiara | Hgsh | C x Diacm x L x Soph |
| Hildaara | Hdra | Bro x Lps x Schom |
| Himoriara | Hmra | Asctm x Phal x Rhy x V |
| Holcoglossum | Hlcgl* | Natural |
| Holttumara | Holtt | Arach x Ren x V |
| Hookerara | Hook | B x C x Diacm |
| Howeara | Hwra | Lchs x Onc x Rdza |
| Hueylihara | Hylra | Neof x Ren x Rhy |
| Hugofreedara | Hgfda | Asctm x Dor x King |
| Hummelara | Humm | Bark x B x Epi |
| Huntleanthes | Hnths | Cnths x Hya |
| Hygrochilus | Hygrch* | Natural |
| Hyntleya | Hya | Natural |

| | | |
|---|---|---|
| Ionettia | Intta | Comp x Inps |
| Ionocidium | Incdm | Inps x Onc |
| Ionopsis | Inps | Natural |
| Irvingara | Irv | Arach x Ren x Trgl |
| Isaoara | Isr | Aer x Asctm x Phal x V |
| Iwanagara | Iwan | B x C x Diacm x L |
| Izumiara | Izma | C x Epi x L x Schom x Soph |
| Jewellara | Jwa | Bro x C x Epi x L |
| Jimenezara | Jmzra | Bro x L x Lps |
| Joannara | Jnna | Ren x Rhy x V |
| Johnkellyara | Jkl | Brs x Lchs x Onc x Rdza |
| Johnyeeara | Jya | B x C x Epi x L x Schom x Soph |
| Jumanthes | Jmth | Aerth x Jum |
| Jumellea | Jum | Natural |
| Kagawara | Kgw | Asctm x Ren x V |
| Kanzerara | Kza | Chdrh x Prom x Z |
| Kawamotoara | Kwmta | B x C x Dga x Epi x L |
| Keferanthes | Kefth | Cnths x Kefst |
| Kefersteinia | Kefst | Natural |
| Kingidium | Kngdm* | Natural |
| Kingiella | King | Natural |
| Kirchara | Kir | C x Epi x L x Soph |
| Klehmara | Klma | Diacm x L x Schom |
| Knappara | Knp | Asctm x Rhy x V x Vdps |
| Knudsonara | Knud | Asctm x Neof x Ren x Rhy x V |
| Komkrisara | Kom | Asctm x Ren x Rhy |
| Kraussara | Krsa | Bro x C x Diacm x Lps |
| Laelia | L | Natural |
| Laeliocatonia | Lctna | Bro x C x L |
| Laeliocattkeria | Lcka | Bark x C x L |
| Laeliocattleya | Lc | C x L |
| Laeliokeria | Lkra | Bark x L |
| Laeliopleya | Lpya | C x Lps |
| Laeliopsis | Lps | Natural |
| Laelonia | Lna | Bro x L |
| Lagerara | Lgra | Asp x Cda x Odm |
| Lancebirkara | Lbka | Bol x Cnths x Pes |
| Lauara | Lauara | Ascgm x Ren x Rhy |
| Laycockara | Lay | Arach x Phal x Vdps |
| Leeara | Leeara | Arach x V x Vdps |
| Lemaireara | Lemra | Bro x Ctps x Epi |
| Leochilus | Lchs | Natural |
| Leocidium | Lcdm | Lchs x Onc |
| Leocidmesa | Lcmsa | Gom x Lchs x Onc |
| Leocidpasia | Lcdpa | Asp x Lchs x Onc |
| Lepanthes | Lths | Natural |
| Leptodendrum | Lrtdm | Epi x Lpt |
| Leptokeria | Lptka | Bark x Lpt |
| Leptolaelia | Lptl | L x Lpt |
| Leptotes | Lpt | Natural |
| Leptovola | Lptv | B x Lpt |
| Leslieara | Lesl | Bro x Ctps x Diacm x Epi |
| Lewisara | Lwsra | Aer x Arach x Asctm x V |
| Liaopsis | Liaps | L x Lps |
| Lichtara | Licht | Dor x Gchls x Phal |
| Liebmanara | Lieb | Asp x Cda x Onc |
| Limara | Lim | Arach x Ren x Vdps |
| Limatodes | Limtd | Natural |
| Lioponia | Lpna | Bro x Lps |
| Lockcidium | Lkcdm | Lhta x Onc |
| Lockhartia | Lhta | Natural |
| Lockochilettia | Lkctta | Comp x Lchs x Lhta |
| Lockochilus | Lkchs | Lchs x Lhta |
| Lockogochilus | Lkgch | Gom x Lchs x Lhta |
| Lockopilia | Lckp | Lhta x Trpla |
| Lockostalix | Lkstx | Lhta x Sgmx |
| Lowara | Low | B x L x Soph |
| Lowsonara | Lwnra | Aer x Asctm x Rhy |
| Luascotia | Lscta | Asctm x Lsa x Neof |
| Ludisia | Lds* | Natural |
| Luicentrum | Lctm | Asctm x Lsa |
| Luichilus | Luic | Lsa x Sarco |
| Luinetia | Lnta | Lsa x Neof |
| Luinopsis | Lnps | Lsa x Phal |
| Luisanda | Lsnd | Lsa x V |
| Luisia | Lsa | Natural |
| Luistylis | Lst | Lsa x Rhy |
| Luivanetia | Lvta | Lsa x Neof x V |
| Lutherara | Luth | Phal x Ren x Rhy |
| Lycaste | Lyc | Natural |
| Lycasteria | Lystr | Bif x Lyc |
| Lymanara | Lynra | Aer x Arach x Ren |
| Lyonara | Lyon | C x L x Soph |
| Maccoyara | Mcyra | Aer x V x Vdps |
| Macekara | Maka | Arach x Phal x Ren x V x Vdps |
| Maclellanara | Mclna | Brs x Odm x Onc |
| Maclemoreara | Mclmra | B x L x Schom |
| Macodes | Mac | Natural |
| Macomaria | Mcmr | Haem x Mac |
| Macradenia | Mcdn | Natural |
| Macradesa | Mcdsa | Gom x Mcdn |

| | | | | | |
|---|---|---|---|---|---|
| Mailamaiara | Mai | C x Diacm x L x Schom | Neostylis | Neost | Neof x Rhy |
| Masdevallia | Masd | Natural | Neogardneria | Ngda | Natural |
| Masonara | Msna | Agn x Btmna x Clx x Otst x Prom x Zspm | Ngara | Ngara | Arach x Ascgm x Ren |
| | | | Nobleara | Nlra | Aer x Ren x V |
| | | | Nonaara | Non | Aer x Ascgm x Ren |
| | | | Nornahamamotoara | Nhmta | Aer x Rhy x Vdps |
| Matsudaara | Msda | Bark x C x L x Soph | Northenara | Nrna | C x Epi x L x Schom |
| Maymoirara | Mymra | C x Epi x Lps | Norwoodara | Nwda | Brs x Milt x Onc x Rdza |
| Maxillacaste | Mxcst | Lyc x Max | | | |
| Maxillaria | Max | Natural | Notylettia | Ntlta | Comp x Nlt |
| Maxilobium | Mxlb | Max x Xyl | Notylia | Ntl | Natural |
| Meiracyllium | Mrclm | Natural | Notylidium | Ntldm | Ntl x Onc |
| Menadenium | Mndnm* | Natural | Notylopsis | Ntlps | Inps x Ntl |
| Mendoncella | Mdcla | Natural | Odontioda | Oda | Cda x Odm |
| Mendosepalum | Mdspl | Mdcla x Zspm | Odontobrassia | Odbrs | Brs x Odm |
| Mexicoa | Mxc* | Natural | Odontocidium | Odcdm | Odm x Onc |
| Micholitzara | Mchza | Aer x Asctm x Neof x V | Odontoglossum | Odm | Natural |
| | | | Odontonia | Odtna | Milt x Odm |
| Micropera | Micr | Natural | Odontopilia | Odpla | Odm x Trpla |
| Milpasia | Mpsa | Asp x Milt | Odontorettia | Odrta | Comp x Odm |
| Milpilia | Mpla | Milt x Trpla | Oeoniella | Oenla | Natural |
| Miltada | Mtad | Ada x Milt | Oerstedella | Orstdl* | Natural |
| Miltadium | Mtadm | Ada x Milt x Onc | Okaara | Okr | Asctm x Ren x Rhy x V |
| Miltassia | Mtssa | Brs x Milt | | | |
| Miltistonia | Mtst | Bapt x Milt | Oncidenia | Oncna | Mcdn x Onc |
| Miltonia | Milt | Natural | Oncidesa | Oncsa | Gom x Onc |
| Miltonidium | Mtdm | Milt x Onc | Oncidettia | Onctta | Comp x Onc |
| Miltonioda | Mtda | Cda x Milt | Oncidiella | Onclla | Onc x Rdzlla |
| Miltonioides | Mltnds* | Natural | Oncidioda | Oncda | Cda x Onc |
| Miltoniopsis | Mltnps* | Natural | Oncidium | Onc | Natural |
| Mizutara | Miz | C x Diacm x Schom | Oncidpilia | Oncpa | Onc x Trpla |
| Moirara | Moir | Phal x Ren x V | Onoara | Onra | Asctm x Ren x V x Vdps |
| Mokara | Mkra | Arach x Asctm x V | | | |
| Monnierara | Monn | Ctsm x Cyc x Morm | Opsisanda | Opsis | V x Vdps |
| Moonara | Mnra | Aer x Asctm x Neof x Rhy | Opsiscattleya | Opsct | C x Ctps |
| | | | Opsistylis | Opst | Rhy x Vdps |
| Mormodes | Morm | Natural | Orchis | Orchis | Natural |
| Mormolyca | Mlca | Natural | Orchiserapias | Orsps | Orchis x Srps |
| Moscosoara | Mscra | Bro x Epi x Lps | Ornithocidium | Orncm | Onc x Orpha |
| Mystacidium | Mycdm | Natural | Ornithophora | Orpha | Natural |
| Nageliella | Ngl | Natural | Osmentara | Osmt | Bro x C x Lps |
| Nakagawaara | Nkgwa | Aer x Dor x Phal | Osmoglossum | Osmgls* | Natural |
| Nakamotoara | Nak | Asctm x Neof x V | Otaara | Otr | B x Bro x C x L |
| Nashara | Nash | Bro x Ctps x Diacm | Otocolax | Otcx | Clx x Otst |
| Naugleara | Naug | Asctm x Ascgm x Ren | Otoglossum | Otglss* | Natural |
| Neobathiea | Nbth | Natural | Otonisia | Otnsa | Agn x Otst |
| Neobatopus | Nbps | Crypt x Nbth | Otosepalum | Otspm | Otst x Zspm |
| Neofinetia | Neof | Natural | Otostylis | Otst | Natural |
| Neoglossum | Neogm | Ascgm x Neof | Owensara | Owsr | Dor x Phal x Ren |
| Neograecum | Ngrcm | Asgcm Neof | Pabstia | Pab | Natural |

| | | | | | | |
|---|---|---|---|---|---|---|
| Pageara | Pga | Asctm x Lsa x Rhy x V | Propetalum | Pptm | Prom x Z |
| Palmerara | Plmra | Btmna x Otst x Zspm | Psychopsis | Psychp* | Natural |
| Pantapaara | Pntp | Ascgm x Ren x V | Pteroceras | Ptrcrs* | Natural |
| Paphiopedilum | Paph | Natural | Pterostylis | Ptst | Natural |
| Papilionanthe | Pplnnt* | Natural | Raganara | Rgn | Ren x Trgl x V |
| Parachilus | Prcls | Psarco x Sarco | Ramasamyara | Rmsya | Arach x Rhy x V |
| Paradisanthus | Pdsnth | Natural | Recchara | Recc | B x C x L x Schom |
| Paraphalaenopsis | Prphln* | Natural | Renades | Rnds | Aer x Ren |
| Parasarcochilus | Psarco | Natural | Renafinanda | Rfnda | Neof x Ren x V |
| Parnataara | Parn | Aer x Arach x Phal | Renaglottis | Rngl | Ren x Trgl |
| Paulara | Plra | Asctm x Dor x Phal | Renancentrum | Rnctm | Asctm x Ren |
| | | x Ren x V | Renanda | Rnnd* | Arach x Ren x V |
| Paulsenara | Plsra | Aer x Arach x Trgl | Renanetia | Rnet | Neof x Ren |
| Pecteilis | Pctls* | Natural | Renanopsis | Rnps | Ren x Vdps |
| Pehara | Peh | Aer x Arach x V x Vdps | Renanstylis | Rnst | Ren x Rhy |
| Pelacentrum | Plctm | Asctm x Pthia | Renantanda | Rntda | Ren x V |
| Pelachilus | Pelcs | Gchls x Pthia | Renanthera | Ren | Natural |
| Pelastylis | Pelst | Pthia x Rhy | Renantherella | Rnnthg* | Natural |
| Pelatantheria | Pthia | Natural | Renanthoglossum | Rngm | Ascgm x Ren |
| Pelatoritis | Pltrs | Dor x Pthia | Renanthopsis | Rnthps | Phal x Ren |
| Perreiraara | Prra | Aer x Rhy x V | Restrepia | Rstp | Natural |
| Pescatobollea | Psbol | Bol x Pes | Rhinerrhiza | Rhin | Natural |
| Pescatorea | Pes | Natural | Rhinochilus | Rhincs | Rhin x Sarco |
| Pescawarrea | Psw | Pes x Wra | Rhynchocentrum | Rhctm | Asctm x Rhy |
| Pescoranthes | Psnth | Cnths x Pes | Rhyncholaelia | Rhynch* | Natural |
| Pettitara | Pett | Ada x Brs x Onc | Rhynchonopsis | Rhnps | Phal x Rhy |
| Phaiocalanthe | Phcal | Cal x Phaius | Rhynchorides | Rhrds | Aer x Rhy |
| Phaiocymbidium | Phcym | Cym x Phaius | Rhynchostylis | Rhy | Natural |
| Phaius | Phaius | Natural | Rhynchovanda | Rhv | Rhy x V |
| Phalaenopsis | Phal | Natural | Rhyndoropsis | Rhdps | Dor x Phal x Rhy |
| Phalaerianda | Phda | Aer x Phal x V | Richardmizutaara | Rcmza | Asctm x Phal x Vdps |
| Phalandopsis | Phdps | Phal x Vdps | Richardsonara | Rchna | Asp x Odm x Onc |
| Phalanetia | Phnta | Neof x Phal | Ridleyara | Ridl | Arach x Trgl x V |
| Phaliella | Phlla | King x Phal | Robifinetia | Rbf | Neof x Rbq |
| Phragmipaphium | Phrphm | Paph x Phrag | Robinara | Rbnra | Aer x Asctm x Ren |
| Phragmipedium | Phrag | Phrag | | | x V |
| Phillipsara | Phill | Cnths x Stenia x Z | Robiquetia | Rbq | Natural |
| Plectochilus | Plchs | Plrhz x Sarco | Rodrassia | Rdssa | Brs x Rdza |
| Plectorrhiza | Plrhz | Natural | Rodrettia | Rdtta | Comp x Rdza |
| Plectrelgraecum | Plgcm | Angcm x Plmths | Rodrettiopsis | Rdtps | Comp x Inps x Rdza |
| Plectrelminthus | Plmths | Natural | Rodrichilus | Rdchs | Lchs x Rdza |
| Polycycnis | Pcn | Natural | Rodricidium | Rdcm | Onc x Rdza |
| Polystachya | Pol | Natural | Rodridenia | Rden | Mcdn x Rdza |
| Pomacentrum | Pmctm | Asctm x Pmcpa | Rodriglossum | Rdgm | Odm x Rdza |
| Pomatisia | Pmtsa | Lsa x Pmcpa | Rodriguezia | Rdza | Natural |
| Pomatocalpa | Pmcpa | Natural | Rodrigueziella | Rdzlla | Natural |
| Potinara | Pot | B x C x L x Soph | Rodriopsis | Rodps | Inps x Rdza |
| Prolax | Prx | Clx x Prom | Rodritonia | Rdtna | Milt x Rdza |
| Promenaea | Prom | Natural | Rolfeara | Rolf | B x C x Soph |

| | | | | | |
|---|---|---|---|---|---|
| Ronnyara | Rnya | Aer x Asctm x Rhy x V | Severinara | Sev | Diacm x L x Soph |
| Rosakirschara | Rskra | Asctm x Neof x Ren | Shigeuraara | Shgra | Asctm x Ascgm x Ren x V |
| Roseara | Rsra | Dor x King x Phal x Ren | Shipmanara | Shipm | Bro x Diacm x Schom |
| Rossioglossum | Rssgls* | Natural | Shiveara | Shva | Asp x Brs x Odm x Onc |
| Rothara | Roth | B x C x Epi x L x Soph | Sidranara | Sidr | Ascrm x Phal x Ren |
| | | | Sigmatostalix | Sgmx | Natural |
| Rotorara | Rtra | Bol x Cnths x Kefst | Silpaprasertara | Silpa | Aer x Asctm x Snths |
| Rudolfiella | Rud | Natural | Sladeara | Slad | Dor x Phal x Sarco |
| Rumrillara | Rlla | Asctm x Neof x Rhy | Sobennigraecum | Sbgcm | Angcm x Sbk |
| Saccolabium | Saccm | Natural | Sobennikoffia | Sbk | Natural |
| Sagarikara | Sgka | Aer x Arach x Rhy | Sobralia | Sob | Natural |
| Sanderara | Sand | Brs x Cda x Odm | Sophrocattleya | Sc | C x Soph |
| Sanjumeara | Sjma | Aer x Neof x Rhy x V | Sophrolaelia | Sl | L x Soph |
| Sappanara | Sapp | Arach x Phal x Ren | Sophrolaeliocattleya | Slc | C x L x Soph |
| Sarcanthus | Snths | Natural | Sophronitella | Sphrnt* | Natural |
| Sarcocentrum | Srctm | Asctm x Sarco | Sophronitis | Soph | Natural |
| Sarcochilus | Sarco | Natural | Spathoglottis | Spa | Natural |
| Sarcomoanthus | Sran | Sarco x Dry | Staalara | Staal | Bark x L x Soph |
| Sarconopsis | Srnps | Phal x Sarco | Stacyara | Stac | C x Epi x Soph |
| Sarcorhize | Srza | Rhin x Sarco | Stamariaara | Stmra | Asctm x Phal x Ren x V |
| Sarcothera | Srth | Ren x Sarco | | | |
| Sarcovanda | Srv | Sarco x V | Stanfieldara | Sfdra | Epi x L x Soph |
| Saridestylis | Srdts | Asr x Rhy x Snths | Stangora | Stga | Gga x Stan |
| Sartylis | Srts | Rhy x Sarco | Stanhocycnis | Stncn | Pcn x Stan |
| Satyrium | Satm | Natural | Stanhopea | Stan | Natural |
| Sauledaara | Sdra | Asp x Brs x Milt x Onc x Rdza | Staurochilus | Stchls* | Natural |
| | | | Stauropsis | Strpss* | Natural |
| Scaphyglottis | Scgl | Natural | Stellamizutaara | Stlma | Bro x Bro x C |
| Schafferara | Schfa | Asp x Brs x Cda x Milt x Odm | Stenia | Stenia | Natural |
| | | | Stewartara | Stwt | Ada x Cda x Odm |
| Schombavola | Smbv | B x Schom | Sutingara | Sut | Arach x Asctm x Phal x V x Vdps |
| Schombocatonia | Smbcna | Bro x C x Schom | | | |
| Schombocattleya | Smbc | C x Schom | Symphoglossum | Sympho* | Natural |
| Schombodiacrium | Smbdcm | Diacm x Schom | Symphyglossum | Symphy* | Natural |
| Schomboepidenrum | Smbep | Epi x Schom | Teohara | Thra | Arach x Ren x V x Vdps |
| Schombolaelia | Smbl | L x Schom | | | |
| Schombonia | Smbna | Bro x Schom | Tetracattleya | Ttct | C x Ttma |
| Schombonitis | Smbts | Schrom x Soph | Tetradiacrium | Ttdm | Diacm x Ttma |
| Schromburgkia | Schom | Natural | Tetrakeria | Ttka | Bark x Ttma |
| Scottara | Sctt | Aer x Arach x Lsa | Tetraliopsis | Ttps | Lps x Ttma |
| Scullyara | Scu | C x Epi x Schom | Tetramicra | Ttma | Natural |
| Seahexa | Sxa | Hex x Hxsa | Tetratonia | Tttna | Bro x Ttma |
| Sedenfadenia | Sdnfda* | Natural | Thelymitra | Thel | Natural |
| Sedirea | Sdr* | Natural | Thesaera | Thsra | Aergs x Aerth |
| Seidenfadenia | Seidnf* | Natural | Thunia | Thu | Natural |
| Selenipedium | Sel | Natural | Trautara | Trta | Dor x Lsa x Phal |
| Serapias | Srps | Natural | Trevorara | Trev | Arach x Phal x V |

| Trichocentrum | Trctm | Natural |
| Trichocidium | Trcdm | Onc x Trctm |
| Trichoglottis | Trgl | Natural |
| Trichonopsis | Trnps | Phal x Trgl |
| Trichopilia | Trpla | Natural |
| Trichopsis | Trcps | Trgl x Vdps |
| Trichostylis | Trst | Rhy x Trgl |
| Trichovanda | Trcv | Trgl x V |
| Trigolyca | Trgca | Mcla x Trgdm |
| Trigonidium | Trgdm | Natural |
| Tubaecum | Tbcm | Angcm x Tblm |
| Tuberolabium | Tblm | Natural |
| Tuckerara | Tuck | C x Diacm x Epi |
| Uptonara | Upta | Phal x Rhy x Sarco |
| Vanalstyneara | Vnsta | Milt x Odm x Onc x Rdza |
| Vancampe | Vcp | Acp x V |
| Vanda | V | Natural |
| Vandachnis | Vchns | Arach x Vdps |
| Vandaenopsis | Vdnps | Phal x V |
| Vandaeranthes | Vths | Aerth x V |
| Vandewegheara | Vwga | Asctm x Dor x Phal x V |
| Vandofinetia | Vf | Neof x V |
| Vandofinides | Vfds | Aer x Neof x V |
| Vandopsides | Vdpsd | Aer x Vdps |
| Vandopsis | Vdps | Natural |
| Vandoritis | Vdts | Dor x V |
| Vanglossum | Vgm | Ascgm x V |
| Vascostylis | Vasco | Asctm x Rhy x V |
| Vaughnara | Vnra | B x C x Epi |
| Vejvarutara | Vja | Bro x C x Ctps |
| Vuylstekeara | Vuyl | Cda x Milt x Odm |
| Warneara | Wnra | Comp x Onc x Rdza |
| Warrea | Wra | Natural |
| Warscewiczella | Wrscwc* | Natural |
| Westara | Wsta | B x Bro x C x L x Schom |
| Wilburchangara | Wbchg | Bro x C x Epi x Schom |
| Wilkinsara | Wknsra | Asctm x V x Vdps |
| Wilsonara | Wils | Cda x Odm x Onc |
| Wingfieldara | Wgfa | Asp x Brs x Odm |
| Withnerara | With | Asp x Milt x Odm x Onc |
| Wooara | Woo | B x Bro x Epi |
| Xylobium | Xyl | Natural |
| Yahiroara | Yhra | B x C x Epi x L x Schom |
| Yamadara | Yam | B x C x Epi X L |
| Yapara | Yap | Phal x Rhy x V |
| Yoneoara | Ynra | Ren x Rhy x Vdps |
| Yonezawaara | Yzwr | Neof x Rhy x V |
| Yusofara | Ysfra | Arach x Asctm x Ren x V |
| Zygobatemannia | Zbm | Btmna x Z |
| Zygocaste | Zcst | Lyc x Z |
| Zygocella | Zcla | Mdcla x Z |
| Zygocolax | Zcx | Clx x Z |
| Zygodisanthus | Zdsnth | Pdsnth x Z |
| Zygolum | Zglm | Z x Zspm |
| Zygoneria | Zga | Ngda x Z |
| Zygonisia | Zns | Agn x Z |
| Zygopetelum | Z | Natural |
| Zygorhyncha | Zcha | Chdra x Z |
| Zygosepalum | Zspm | Natural |
| Zygostylis | Zsts | Otst x Z |
| Zygotorea | Zgt | Pes x Z |
| Zygowarrea | Zwr | Wra x Z |